Keep Off the Grass

Praise for Keep Off the Grass

'A racy and entertaining account of a romp through an ever-changing yet timeless India… wild, witty and wicked!'

—Ruskin Bond

'Gripping, captivating, surreal and believable.'

—Ben Rekhi, international award-winning director

'An unlikely, remarkable story… It's well worth following Ratan on his journey from New York's high life to incarceration in India.'

—*Publishers Weekly*

'A most interesting and unusual pursuit… a fascinating and entertaining look at life in India.'

—*Amazon Top Reviewer*

'Pacy, unpretentious and great fun to read!'

—*Outlook*

'Wild and racy… a huge success.'

—*Hindu*

'Endearing and likeably self deprecating.'

—*Business Standard*

Keep Off the Grass

KARAN BAJAJ

HarperCollins *Publishers* India
a joint venture with

New Delhi

First published in India in 2008 by
HarperCollins *Publishers* India
a joint venture with
The India Today Group

Copyright © Karan Bajaj 2008

ISBN: 978-81-7223-756-1

7th impression, 2010

Karan Bajaj asserts the moral right to be identified
as the author of this book.

HarperCollins *Publishers*
A-53, Sector 57, NOIDA, Uttar Pradesh – 201301, India
77-85 Fulham Palace Road, London W6 8JB, United Kingdom
Hazelton Lanes, 55 Avenue Road, Suite 2900, Toronto, Ontario M5R 3L2
and 1995 Markham Road, Scarborough, Ontario M1B 5M8, Canada
25 Ryde Road, Pymble, Sydney, NSW 2073, Australia
31 View Road, Glenfield, Auckland 10, New Zealand
10 East 53rd Street, New York NY 10022, USA

Typeset in 10.5/15 Adobe Caslon Pro
Jojy Philip New Delhi 110 015

Printed and bound at
Thomson Press (India) Ltd.

To my parents, in health and happiness

'These are the days that must happen to you:
You shall not heap up what is called riches,
You shall scatter with lavish hand all that you earn
or achieve,
You but arrive at the city to which you were
destined—you hardly settle yourself to
satisfaction, before you are called by an irresistible
call to depart.'

—Walt Whitman, *Song of the Open Road*, Verse 11

1

An Irresistible Call to Depart

'Let me guess, you're a Cancer, right?' asked Christine, a look of frank curiosity in her hazel eyes.

I gazed at her in incomprehension as I tried to recall the details of our encounter last night. I thought we had met at a bar in the Upper West Side, but it could well have been Chelsea. Damn, this was embarrassing. No, wait, got it. We met past midnight at the after-party in Peter's apartment. She was a Broadway actress who had a thing for bankers, and we had had a glorious, phoney discussion about a new art gallery.

I felt proud of myself. Despite being inebriated, I had probably succeeded in sounding pretentious enough to get an invitation back to her apartment. I felt even prouder to note that my performance hadn't suffered because of the alcohol. Otherwise why would we be here, enjoying our morning-after, having sushi for brunch in this fancy new Asian-Latino fusion restaurant? But what was this 'Cancer' business? Gosh, had I been so pathetic as to call out for my doctor father or some other Freudian tripe like that? I was about to ask her for an explanation when I overheard snippets of conversation from the table next to ours.

'Don't you just love this place? It's so... so ethnic,' gushed a middle-aged platinum blonde to her identical-looking friend. 'I thought I had outgrown sushi, but this place is just, like, so totally awesome.'

'I'm breaking up with Richard,' her friend replied, paying no attention to the sushi comment. 'I think I love him, but I'm not, like, *in* love with him, if you know what I mean.'

I pulled myself away from their profound exchange to observe Christine daintily sample her Kodako Nigiri.

'Sushi got your tongue?' smiled Christine, brushing a wisp of golden blonde hair away from her face with the back of her hand. I knew she thought she looked adorable when she did that. 'If it isn't Cancer, then it's definitely Gemini,' she said.

All of a sudden, I was tired. I didn't belong here. Zodiac signs, twenty-year-old ditzy actresses, fusion restaurants, baby octopus for lunch, miniature brioche buns for dinner, independent movies, art galleries, outgrowing sushi, breaking up with Richard—none of it was real. Rather, all of it was real. I was fake, the impostor who didn't belong here. The same eerie feeling of living someone else's life was haunting me again. I'm drowning, I wanted to shout, someone please throw me a fucking stick.

'Did you say something, big boy?' she asked.

Oh Christine, I thought, the only sign I can think of right now is the Ram. I want us to get back to your apartment and go at it until I can't think any more because thinking, you see, is dangerous; too much of it drives even sane people insane.

'Cancer,' I mumbled. 'Right the first time.'

'That's what I told Richard. I really need to find out who *I* am first,' floated the voice from the next table.

That's it, I thought, I'm done. I began thumbing down my BlackBerry. Sadly, one of the few benefits of being a banker was that everyone expected you to be an asshole.

'I need to rush,' I said. 'Something's come up. Do you mind if we do this some other time?'

Christine must have been shocked by my rudeness. Later, I felt bad that I didn't give her enough time to clean up the Uni-Tama on her plate. After all, she was the unlikely silicone angel who had compelled me, the Yale-educated, American-born, pampered son of immigrant Indian parents to quit my cushy Wall Street investment-banking job and leave Manhattan. But I was in a hurry that day. Soon there would be significant departures from the neat, tight script of my life and some scenes needed to be rewritten immediately.

✻

Monday morning. As usual, my alarm went off at 5 a.m., the same time it had buzzed every weekday in the past twenty-odd years of my existence. Mornings were always busy: In high school, I woke up early to attend violin classes because Dad was convinced you needed something 'extra' for admission to Yale or Harvard; in Yale, I got up to maintain my place in the athletics squad because investment banks viewed participation in competitive sports favourably in their interviews; now, waking up early ensured that I was the first analyst to reach the bank.

I switched off the alarm, picked up my BlackBerry and scrolled down the messages sleepily. The usual Monday morning 'Urgent' e-mails about pitch books and client meetings; today though, my attention drifted to the Zen footers at the bottom of the e-mails.

Carpe diem. Seize the day.

Life is too short to not smell the flowers that bloom at your feet.

Life isn't complicated, you make it so.

Jesus, did people *really* believe this smack? I got a surprise for you, buster: it is complicated. You hurt those you love the most; the bigger an asshole you are, the better you do in life; you strive for all the things that don't matter and let go of things that matter the most. Try telling the Chinese sweatshop worker, who is going blind from sewing Nikes, to seize the day, or the gutter cleaners in India to smell the roses. It is simple, isn't it? I put the BlackBerry down. But I couldn't make myself get up from the bed. I lolled around for a couple of hours, smoking a smooth Dunhill and staring blankly at the Monet and Warhol replicas on the walls of my studio apartment. Soft music from an acoustic guitar instrumental played in the background on the Bang and Olufsen music system.

The cell phone beeped. A message from Christine: 'Had fun stallion. The opera this weekend?'

I smiled. I had created an elaborate sham of a life. Fake Monets, acoustic guitar instrumentals, SMS invites to the New York opera—none of these belonged here, the same way I didn't belong. I pulled the soft, luxurious cover to my chin, staring at the ceiling as the random idea that had struck me over lunch with Christine began to take shape. By the time I finally made my way to my office on Wall Street, it was 8 a.m.

The fiftieth floor of the tallest building on Wall Street, plush furniture in the lobby, a gorgeous receptionist with a Brit accent and a plunging neckline, the latest Fazzino on the walls. It had all seemed so impressive two years ago, I thought as I walked over to my cubicle. Just what had happened?

'Here he comes,' exclaimed Peter as I switched on my computer. Peter was my closest friend from Yale and partly by fortitude and partly by intent, we had ended up in the same firm—he after taking a couple of years off to back-pack across Thailand, Vietnam and Cambodia, me after abandoning my PhD in physics halfway at Yale.

'Dude, are you all right? 'Coz this is the first time I've beaten you to work or class since we've known each other. I was worried maybe the actress showed you a different movie, or should I say move, from the one you expected.' He winked.

'I'm fine, I'll fill you in later, okay? Has Ruth asked for me yet?' I said.

'Yes, of course,' said Peter. 'Her star protégé, her shining diamond has never showed up at work later than seven in the a.m., so yeah, she has been hopping around for a while. She's worried you might develop a life outside work. Of course, she doesn't know about your weekend adventures yet. Speak of the devil…'

I turned around to see Ruth, my tall, blonde, hard-driven Australian manager, arriving with a sheaf of important-looking papers in her hand. It was business as usual. Banks didn't know or care about crises of the soul.

I spent the rest of the day (and most of the night) filling in spreadsheet after spreadsheet for a meeting with an important client, a major apparel manufacturer that earned a majority of its profits from its underwear collection. During the course of the next fifteen hours, I became an expert on what different types of underwear cost, which US retailers sold half-priced underwear, what size underwear was the most profitable to produce, how economic recession impacted underwear consumption, which colour underwear were the most popular at Christmas and other such important, fascinating facts. At two in the morning, I finally sent the analyses to Ruth, swearing I would set my plan in motion immediately. I never had lofty ambitions for myself, and I didn't care if there was a different destiny waiting for me somewhere else. All I knew was that becoming a connoisseur of the underwear industry hadn't figured in my list of childhood ambitions.

My phone rang just as I was about to head off to Peter's cubicle.

'Good work, Samrat,' said Ruth. A kid yelled in the background. 'Take fifty prints for tomorrow's alignment meeting at seven, will you? Spiral bound.'

The kid squealed louder as if it was being sacrificed at the altar. 'Mommy is on the phone, honey,' said Ruth in the same voice she used to speak to Peter.

Suddenly, I didn't want to end up like her. President of a white-collar sweatshop, hundred-hour work weeks, pre-meetings for alignment meetings for pre-meetings to the client meetings, spiral-bound pitch books at two in the morning, squealing kids, indifferent spouse, demanding clients.

'And let's squeeze ten minutes out of my calendar

tomorrow to talk about your business school application,' she said.

I could accurately predict every day of the next twenty years of my life, I thought as I fired the prints. From associate to analyst to Harvard Business School to vice-president to managing director; a wife, two kids, a nanny and a housekeeper; a summer house in the Hampton's; a vacation home in Colorado; sell off the summer house in a financial crisis, buy two in a boom. Variation would mean being promoted six months earlier or later; and going to Wharton instead of Harvard.

I wasn't meant for this, I thought as I began spiral binding the pitch book. This isn't the life I chose, I am living someone else's reality.

'Fancy a smoke?' I asked Peter as I stepped into his cubicle after leaving the pitch books in a neat pile on Ruth's table. He was surfing porn, short, thickset body bent over the keyboard, one hand on his bald pate, the other typing on the keyboard furiously. He looked more like a skinhead than a banker, I thought, and he definitely did behave like one. Who else would be up at 2 a.m., not for a noble cause like tracking a client's financial position, but to follow Jenna Jameson's favourite positions?

'Just a minute,' he said, turning to me. His blue eyes sparkled with excitement. 'I'm on the verge of a breakthrough. Check out this site.'

I nodded appreciatively, wondering for the

millionth time since meeting him six years back at Yale just how he managed to get by.

'Done,' he said, getting up from his chair. 'Let's pack up. Another busy day.'

We made our way out of the quiet building, shivering in the crisp winter air. The neon sign of the Chinese take-out place flashed at the corner of the quiet street.

'I'm leaving,' I said as we lit our cigarettes.

A bum was shivering outside the unlit Starbucks. Fancy telling him, I thought, that I was about to quit my quarter-million-dollar-paying investment banking job because I was feeling 'empty'. He'd probably stick the needle he had in his hand into my eyes.

'Bad day, eh?' said Peter.

'No. I'm serious. I'm quitting,' I said.

'Dude, don't give me that. Not you,' said Peter. 'You're meant for this. Straight As in high school, perfect SAT, 4.0 in Yale, athlete of the year, Ruth's darling errand boy, this place runs on screwed-up folks like you.'

'Whatever,' I said. 'I'm done.'

Big stoned eyes narrowed in disbelief. 'And where are you heading? Private equity?' he said.

'No, definitely not. I think I'll probably go back to completing my PhD. I kind of liked it. Maybe get back in academia after that, become a professor or something,' I said.

'Bull,' Peter said. 'You aren't interested in the PhD, you just want to get back to the old life. Look, get over it. No one does their first job forever.'

'See, this is what I'm tired of. This whole… whole Truman show,' I said. 'Everybody has an opinion on my life. Play the violin, score As in school, participate in athletics, go to Yale, become a doctor or a banker, apply to Harvard Business School, don't stick to your first job—everyone seems to be living my life except me.'

'You are Asian, man, this is your destiny.' He laughed.

I didn't laugh.

'Dude,' said Peter. 'Don't get me wrong. I think it's great to quit, this is the crappiest job in the world. Both you and I know that I'm gonna get thrown out soon as well. I just don't think leaving for that PhD is wise, though. You didn't like the course. You didn't even like physics at Yale for that matter. Being good at something doesn't mean you like it. And you're good at this banking bullshit.'

I stared at him. Sometimes he made sense.

'Take some time off. See the world, backpack, hike, travel, find yourself,' he continued. 'Join me. It will give me a reason as well. I am getting restless again.'

Most times, though, he didn't make any sense.

A couple of hours later, I made my way back to my apartment. Talking with Peter hadn't helped much. With a few logical words, he had destroyed the one fantasy that had kept me afloat for the past few months. If I wasn't going back to complete my PhD, what would I do?

'How long have you been here?' asked the bearded Sikh cab driver in Hindi.

This was the last thing I needed. I debated whether to pretend I didn't understand, but I began to feel bad for him. If there was one thing worse than banking, it was probably driving a cab through the lonely streets at three in the morning.

'Just a few years,' I said.

'Do you plan to go back?' he said.

He had touched a raw nerve. 'I don't know,' I said.

'Don't think so much. You should go back,' he said forcefully. 'If I was your age, I would go back.'

Now, what was this about? I felt like I was in a bad CIA movie. How did he know about the conversation I'd just had with Peter?

'It's lonely out here,' he continued. 'The older you get, the lonelier it gets. Go back now while you're still young.'

'It's lonely everywhere,' I said.

He turned around and stared at me in disbelief. 'Not at home, boss, not at home. Even if you have no one, you will find friends and family like *this* in India.' He snapped his fingers. 'No one is lonely in India. You should go back.'

Of course, he had mistaken me for an Indian.

I didn't feel like giving an explanation, so I kept quiet.

'Everything is not thought from the head,' he said, thumping his chest with one hand and swerving dangerously with the other. 'Sometimes, think from the heart as well.'

＊

Three weeks later, I braced myself for a painful discussion and called my father at work.

'Is everything okay, beta?' he asked, sounding very concerned. 'What happened?'

Ours was not a relationship given to sudden, unplanned expressions of love. Like everything else in my strictly ordered life, my weekly phone call to my parents happened on schedule every Sunday evening. A phone call outside that timing usually signified a crisis, and I knew my father would have probably pulled himself out of a surgery to take my call. Heck, I thought, he was Kentucky's best damned cardiac surgeon, after all. He could fix any arterial damage my phone call had caused.

'Everything is fine, Dad. I'm going to... going to India, actually,' I replied hesitantly.

I could almost hear him relax, and my heart warmed to him. He was a simple, uncomplicated man, full of goodness. He wanted nothing more than my happiness. Happiness, I thought to myself, fleeting, elusive happiness, that's all I want too.

'That's great, beta. You haven't been there in so many years, and it's always fun to travel to India on business. Have you told Ma about it yet? She will be overjoyed. Listen, I'm in the middle of something. Why don't I call you in the evening?' he said.

'This isn't a business trip, actually. I'm quitting Goldman and going to India for a couple of years,' I said.

Deafening silence.

I rushed to fill the gap. 'I'm not becoming a hippie, Dad. I'm planning to go to business school there. I've already applied and been accepted.'

Still no response.

'It isn't that bad,' I continued, trying to believe it myself, 'with India becoming an economic superpower and stuff. And an international business degree would probably help my banking career when I'm back... Are you still there?'

'But why would you do that?' he said finally.

'A cabbie told me to,' I said.

'What?' he said.

Where do I start, I thought, *and will you ever understand? For one, I hate the script. I'm twenty-five years old and more than a third of my way through, and I have acted perfectly so far without ever asking for even a single extra take. I've scored straight As in school, become the valedictorian at Yale and joined the best bank on Wall Street. But I can't live this Truman Show any longer. I dislike the monotonous predictability of my life. I'm tired of making a livelihood filling spreadsheets that help make rich, fat bastards richer and even more miserable than they already are. Every day I get the sinking feeling that I'm not creating anything; I'm just pushing paper around. I'm done with the eighteen-hour workdays, and I don't need the constant unnecessary ball-crushing stress to make my first million before thirty. You won't understand this, Dad, but I don't give a flying fuck whether I become a millionaire by thirty or thirty-six, or even if I don't become one at all. I've realized that I'm just not Indian enough to run the race. Can you please try to understand that?*

What I really want to do is to shave my head, grow a beard, become a hippie, wander around Africa and India for a year and 'find myself'. But I'm just not American enough to do that. I'm an ABCD, an American Born Confused Desi, if you will; I can't function without back-up plans, career options and safety nets. So I'm taking the safer route and joining business school in India instead. At least there I can still play the American searching for himself while getting an education that would be somewhat valued by Corporate America.

I know these are the vague, spoiled concerns of the 'privileged Americans', as you say, but I'm one of them now, am I not?

'Samrat? Hello? Are you still there?'

'Yes,' I said. 'I don't know, Dad. I just hate it here.'

'You should have listened to me when I told you to join medical school. But no, you didn't like medicine,' he said. 'Why India, though? Have all the business schools here shut down? After Yale, you should go to Harvard or Stanford, not some school in India.'

'I need a break from here, Dad,' I said. 'Plus, the whole "second-generation immigrant finding his roots in India" is so glamorous now, I think it will work to my advantage. Differentiate my resume and stuff.'

This was true, although I couldn't care less about my resume or my career right now. All the group presidents in the bank and their diamond-studded wives had wept their stone hearts out after seeing *Bend It Like Beckham* and *Bride and Prejudice* and similar nonsense. If I could tell them with a straight face that I had gone to India to find my roots, their eyes would probably well over as they handed me my job back.

'It's going to be okay, Dad. I'm joining the Indian Institute of Management in Bangalore, not Sholapur Leadership Institute, so hopefully you will think there is still some hope. I managed to sneak in through the foreign national quota,' I said lightly.

Dad didn't seem to think it was funny, though.

'Beta, twenty-seven years ago I graduated from a similar college in India and came here to give you a better life. Now you want to go back to the place where I began? Ultimately, it is your decision, though. We will be supportive of whatever you decide to do,' he said tiredly.

Surprisingly, his support made me feel irritated instead of grateful. I wished he would shout, shake me by my shoulders, tell me that it was a wrong decision and forbid me to go. Suddenly, I didn't want to be an adult, to deviate from the script or be held accountable for my choices any more. But my slide down that slippery slope had begun, and there would be no going back now.

I spent my last few weeks in the US wrapping up my affairs and communicating my decision to those who mattered. The reactions ranged from encouragement, albeit the Australian variety, from Ruth ('I am disappointed, but go for it.' No drama. 'We'll be glad to have you back when this foolishness is over.') to disappointment from Mom ('This is what happens when you stay alone for so long. At your age, your father had you. As usual, you're running away from responsibility.') to outright admiration from Peter ('Good for you, dude, you finally stuck it to the Man. I'm very proud of you. And yeah, if your Asian roots screwed you over, you should find out what it's all about. Remember Tarantino: if someone stuck a red-hot poker up your ass, you've got to find out whose name is on the handle.')

I was glad they understood in their own ways, though I still wasn't sure what I was getting into. Hopefully, there were more answers than questions in India, and it wouldn't all be a waste.

2

It's All a Waste

I didn't understand the finality of my decision until I was comfortably strapped into my seat on the twenty-two-hour-long flight from New York to Bangalore with a stopover in Paris.

'That's it,' I thought as the flight took off, 'no turning back now.' And surprisingly, I found myself getting into the zone of not caring pretty quickly. I usually get into that zone when things are neither definitively good nor bad: they just are. Now, for instance, the good (excitement at going to India, escaping the monotony of my life in Manhattan) balanced the bad (a risky, directionless career move, the prospect of two wasted years). But there was so much noise in my head that it genuinely didn't matter any more.

To hell with it, I thought, you get one life, and everyone is allowed a couple of mistakes. Who can predict the future and in the broad scheme of things, does it really matter anyway? Do what you feel like and hope that it sticks. If it doesn't, throw it again. Maybe it will stick the next time round. And if it doesn't, who cares? It's just one insignificant life wasted in the vast ocean of lives all around. Whatever floats your boat, whatever cranks your tractor, whatever melts your butter, whatever humps your camel, whatever sizzles your bacon, whatever tickles your pickle...

I was so spaced out by the time I was on my connecting flight from Paris that I broke my rule of not swapping life stories with the guy sitting in the next seat. No good can ever come of that. At best, you walk away feeling thankful because you met another fucker in the vast cosmos whose world is even more screwed up than yours; at worst, you meet a self-satisfied prick who makes you doubt your life's choices. Unfortunately, it was going to be the latter this time.

'Are you out of your mind?' asked the young Indian software engineer dude sitting next to me on the flight. He wasn't being facetious. He seemed genuinely agitated by my decision to quit Wall Street and go to India for an MBA. With the typical Indian gift for immediate familiarity, he had quickly dispensed with the pleasantries and probed into the intimate details of my life. He now felt compelled to pass judgement on my choices.

He took off his glasses and squinted at me for a while.

Finally, he said, 'You'll be fucked there.' He breathed on the lenses and wiped them on his shirt before putting them back on and continuing, 'Look, I don't mean to sound insulting, but you're what we call a "coconut" in India—brown on the outside, white on the inside. You have grown up in the US and can't even begin to understand how screwed up our Indian education system is.'

He immediately dismissed my suggestion that investment banking on Wall Street wasn't a cakewalk either.

'I don't think you're quite getting it. How do I explain this? The folks in the Indian Institute of Management, they are… how do I put it… crazy behenchods. They have dreamt all their lives of breaking free from the mythical iron hand of the Indian system that grips your balls the moment you are born into the great Indian middle class. There is no place for Yale's "balanced perspectives", "broadened horizons", "work-life balance" and other oestrogen-boosting "let us help you get in touch with yourself" stuff at the IIM. There is only one perspective there: get the highest-paying job. People work like dogs, backstab, front-stab, side-stab— whatever it takes to achieve that. Every year there are cases of suicide.'

I could already feel a cold grip on my balls, but he continued relentlessly.

'Look brother, if you still have the chance, just opt out. Live your high life in Manhattan. Save this self-discovery for another life. It is all maya anyway, the chasing of an illusion. How far do you want to travel to realize that dissatisfaction is the nature of existence and unanswered questions the only real answer?' he said, ending on a surprisingly philosophical note.

The chance conversation would come back to haunt me at various times over the course of the next two years in India. How far did I really need to go before I realized the futility of my journey?

For now, though, there was no time for second thoughts, or first thoughts for that matter, considering how little time I had invested in this decision. The flight had touched down. I was in Bangalore already, the outsourcing capital of the world and the subject of recent frenzied worldwide debates as it threatened to make the US workforce redundant. However, if the famed technological boom had caused any change in living standards, it wasn't apparent. We were greeted by the customary delay at the airport as multiple flights arrived simultaneously and the immigration queue got longer and longer.

'Bastards! Why the hell is it taking them so long to check the papers?' grumbled my engineer friend. 'Who wants to immigrate to India illegally anyway? Bangladeshis only! And will they arrive from New York on an Air France flight?'

More frustration as an immigration officer decided to leave for his mandatory cigarette and tea break, exhausted by the unexpected exertion that the night had thrust upon him. Expletives filled the air: 'Saale sab haraami kaamchor hain', 'everybody is a fucking bastard'.

'See, for you, all this must be charming. The authentic Indian experience that you are seeking in your quixotic trip. However, I promise that if you stay long enough, this kind of stuff will start messing with your head. How can we keep caressing our balls with stories of globalization when even our most basic infrastructure is so hopeless?' ranted my bitter friend.

I didn't find this oft-romanticized sight 'charming' in the least. I wasn't Paul Theroux or Mark Twain or even Patrick Swayze, out here to experience the City of Joy and pontificate on the plight of humanity. I was just another ordinary traveller on an un-heroic journey; one more lost soul in the sea of lost faces around me, out to fill a known void with an unknown one. But I didn't mention this to my friend who was close to breaking point anyway. He seemed to be waging his own private war against the system and cheered up after scowling at the immigration officer who checked his papers. He offered to give me a ride to the Indian Institute of Management.

'My car is outside. It's horribly expensive and unsafe to keep the car parked there during a long trip, but I have an arrangement with the parking lot guys. They watch it and don't charge me the full rates.

In India, everyone has some kind of arrangement or another,' he explained. 'You stay here, I'll be back in one second.'

Waiting outside Arrivals, it felt like I'd stepped into a riot. I'd forgotten what it felt like. A cacophony of sounds, people everywhere as far as the eye could see, stale air smelling of automobile smoke, industrial exhaust and strong tobacco, blaring horns, a swarm of frenzied taxi-drivers descending on me to wrestle my bags away, more shouting, screaming and cursing. A taste of India, I thought, would I really be able to survive two years here away from the creature comforts of the US?

Soon enough, a small bright red car pulled over. My friend got out to help me load my bags. As I squeezed myself in beside him, I immediately detected the sweet smell of marijuana. Then I noticed the dreamy look in his red eyes and the conspiratorial expression on his face.

'Need a joint whenever I get to the airport, man, otherwise the traffic gets to me,' he explained apologetically. 'Don't worry, it won't impact my driving. I have a couple every day in the morning before I drive to work.' Was that supposed to make me feel better?

I wondered whether I should get a cab instead, but Dad's words came to mind. Much to Ma's dismay, he had relented to give me some rare fatherly advice just before I left:

'Now that you have decided to go, beta, here is my only piece of advice. Learn to let go in India. Succumb to India. I always felt that America makes you very soft and self-centred. India will make you a man if you allow it to.'

I decided to be a man and entered his car.

'Would you like to have a joint as well?' he said.

Sure, why not? That's why I'd just left my quarter-million-dollar Wall Street job. To smoke marijuana in India, be driven along the madness of Indian roads with a stoned driver whose hands trembled as they gripped the steering wheel, and possibly end my inglorious pursuit before it even started. A speeding truck, a stoned driver, both passenger and driver killed instantaneously—it was probably a typical Indian story that wouldn't even grace the inside pages of the local newspaper.

'Yes, of course,' I said aloud. *I'm going to make you very proud today, Dad.*

Soon we were flying, and I revelled in my friend's acute observations as he drove the car at Formula One speed over narrow roads. I concentrated on looking straight ahead, into blinding headlights.

'It's all a waste,' he said.

'What is?' I looked around, wondering if I had missed something on the road.

'All of this!' he shouted, agitated at my shallowness. 'Every fucking inch of this.' He removed both hands from the steering wheel and waved at the passing world. The car nearly swerved off the road. 'Lies, hypocrisy, sleaze; it's all around you. They teach their kids to bomb airplanes but won't let them write fuck on the walls.'

'Okay, okay, got it,' I said hastily. 'You're right. It's a waste. Everything is.'

We drove in silence for a while, racing big SUVs, all inexplicably white, when suddenly the road became very bumpy indeed. The seatbelt was broken, so I had to hold on tightly to my seat to avoid hitting the ceiling.

'Fitting,' he said.

'What?' I asked.

'This is the approach road to the IIM. It's falling apart,' he said slowly.

'What's fitting about that?' I asked, puzzled.

He threw his head back and laughed. The car took another dangerous turn. 'It's metaphorical, allegorical, whatever.'

It didn't make any sense, but I said nothing, worried he would lose control of the car.

'The world. It's falling apart,' he said suddenly after a long silence, as we pulled up at a tall, imposing gate. 'We live, we breathe, we pay mortgage, we die, just chasing wind and trying to catch the rainbow.'

I wondered what had inspired this outburst. The entrance to the institute looked harmless enough—warm white gates, an Indian Institute of

Management sign lazily perched on a spire, and a lush green approach to the main building.

'Best of luck, man,' my friend said as he dropped me off. 'Always remember, nothing matters. It's a cosmic conspiracy.'

By now, the dope had hit me as well. We both giggled hysterically. I bade him farewell, delighted at the fact that we hadn't even exchanged names during the past twenty-four hours of knowing each other. Nor e-mail addresses, telephone numbers or promises to meet again. There was nothing fake about our encounter. And I was finally ready to live my own life. I giggled again. This was India, things were probably real here.

3

Things Were Real Here

Would I have chosen a different room in the hostel if had not been stoned that night? Probably.

My tiresome Type-A traits would have kicked in. I would have checked multiple rooms, analysed their pros and cons and probably chosen a bigger room than the small one I had drifted into. But then, would I ever have run into Shine Sarkar at the IIM? At Yale, Peter had once stumbled into my room high as a kite and said, 'Dude, it's all connected!' before passing out on the floor. I had thought nothing of the comment at that time, and had resumed my studies as usual after dragging him to his bed.

But now I thought I understood what he meant. In a sense, everything that happened in India followed a well-laid-out master plan, though it seemed like a series of random events to start with. Or perhaps, it was a death wish of some sort: I had probably been seeking out disaster from the moment I arrived here.

It started with a loud, insolent knock on my door that jolted me awake the next morning. My head hurt from the combined effect of the jetlag, the airport ordeal and the late-night marijuana romp. I woke up confused. Why were the walls of my room covered with crumbling, pale whitewash, and where was the Monet? But it didn't take me long to get back my bearings. With what I would later recognize as disrespect for personal space, so characteristic of life here, a small, dark Bilbo Baggins-esque character, who seemed to be in unusually good humour, barged into my room as soon as I opened the door.

'Ah! You are the famous firang who is going to live next to me. I must say I'm disappointed, though. I was expecting the real deal, a gora—a white-skinned Archie with hairless skin, red hair and freckles on his nose,' he said, plonking himself down on my bed. 'But you, my friend, you look even more Indian than I do. A six-foot plus, broad-shouldered brown giant: Shiva's very own phallic symbol of Indian manhood. Don't worry, I know I'm making no sense. I'm Sarkar by the way—Shine Sarkar, your next-door neighbour.'

I tried to figure out if he was drunk. He didn't seem to be.

'I'm Samrat Ratan,' I mumbled, trying to adjust to this new, undesired presence in my room. 'How do you know I'm from the US?'

'Thank God, at least the accent is authentic and Samrat sounds like a real hippie name. And your red eyes do betray a true jetlag. You are a major celebrity already, firang. Everybody is talking about the Manhattan-based investment banker from Wall Street who has decided to grace us with his presence at the IIM,' he said.

I was surprised. 'What? Why? That hardly warrants star status.'

'You have to understand,' Sarkar said. 'They won't show you this in the Hollywood films about the slums and whores of real India, but becoming an investment banker on Wall Street is the kind of fantasy that adolescent wet dreams are made of in India. And you decided to leave all that and come here; you are the star of the great Indian middle-class porn blockbuster.'

He jabbered on. 'I think you need an authentic Indian cigarette to wake you up. Here, have a Wills Navy Cut. It won't help you win friends or get laid as the ads show, but it will definitely wake you up.'

He was right. It was harsh, quite unlike the Dunhill Lights I smoked in Manhattan, and screamed cancer. The smoke burnt its way down my throat, slowly waking me up in a few drags.

We walked out of the room and I was immediately struck by the sharp, uneven beauty of the IIM campus. The view from our shared balcony was straight out of those sucker tourist postcards that people put up as wallpaper on their desktop. Directly in front of the student hostel was a courtyard with hibiscus and gulmohur trees, not flowering but not completely bare either. Behind us was an Olympic-size playground with a basketball arena, a mini-soccer field and even a skating rink. ('Is that a goddamn skating area?' Sarkar said, equally taken aback as his eyes followed mine, but for different reasons. 'What kind of a wimp skates in India?') The main institute building adjoining the residential hostel seemed to be some sort of a neo-impressionist architectural marvel. From the distant view we got from our balcony, it seemed like cubes were placed over each other to form a complex castle-like structure. I'm usually suspicious of people who climax at seeing oddly shaped buildings and say stuff like 'great endeavour of the mind' or 'victory of the human spirit'. But this view of the imposing building moved me. Not to the point of having an earth-shattering orgasm or anything, but still, it was impressive.

'What? You thought all of India was like Gandhi's ashram?' said Sarkar at my obvious surprise.

I felt ashamed. He was right. I was behaving like a redneck tourist from Kentucky (which I was).

Still, I wasn't too far off the mark, as I would learn later. The campus stood oasis-like amidst the crumbling infrastructure outside. While potholed roads that ensure a bone-breaking ride are not unusual in India, the road leading to the sprawling IIM campus was a real mother. During one particularly harsh monsoon, a visiting professor from Romania or some other exotic eastern European country received a little more than the authentic Indian experience he was seeking when his airport cab sputtered and died on the flooded road. He had to wade his way through shoulder-high water to reach the campus. And if that wasn't enough, the unlucky bastard went on to collide with a floating, dead buffalo and lost his laptop in the ensuing chaos. After shaking off the sordid memories of his introduction to the IIM, he must have wondered how the best business school in the country could be so oblivious to the management problems that abounded in its immediate environment. But as we would soon discover, that precisely was the unofficial motto of the denizens of the business school: 'Ensure your own house is in perfect order even if everything around you is in a shambles.'

Sarkar perched himself on the balcony ledge smoking a cigarette, clearly enjoying the pleasant summer breeze.

'So, where'd you go to school? What's your story?' I asked him.

'Not even mildly as interesting as yours, firang. Mine is the typical Indian story, similar I would presume to almost everyone else's here. No clear ambition, no governing interests. Just drifting along, doing things I'm supposed to be doing, collecting degrees along the way. I had an engineering degree before I came here, though I must admit I'm a horrible engineer. I can't even screw on a light bulb, but thanks to the wretchedness of our education system, I graduated with honours from the IIT.'

An honours student from the Indian Institute of Technology? I knew enough about those to know that he was way smarter than he claimed to be. His story was not too different from mine, though. I had done physics at Yale by default, and had realized my complete inaptitude for it before drifting into a soulless banking job.

I was about to tell him that when we heard a shrill voice call out from behind, 'Hey guys! Are you going for lunch?'

It belonged to a small, bespectacled guy with thinning hair as oily as his smile. 'Myself Chetan Sharma from Mumbai, chartered accountant. I heard you were an investment banker in New York. I wanted to make an introduction.'

Word travels fast in India, I thought. We made the perfunctory introductions. Once the smile was gone, Chetan had a worried, anxious look on his face. I didn't want to judge him too harshly and so soon, but he did resemble the Gollums on Wall Street: bankers whose obsession with their year-end bonus rivalled the fixation of the legendary Tolkien character. Or as Brad Pitt (more eloquent, in my opinion, than Tolkien) said in *Fight Club:* 'The things that they own start owning them.'

Over the course of the conversation, Chetan gave a disinterested Sarkar and a somewhat fascinated me a detailed description of his scoring 'always 90 per cent at least' in school, which I guessed meant straight As, his acing the prestigious National Chartered Accountancy examination and his frustration at being rejected by the Indian Institute of Management at Ahmedabad, arguably the best of the IIMs. 'Chutiyas. The interviewers were asking too many personal questions on soft stuff like listening skills, sensitivity, etc. Are they interviewing me to be an investment banker or a call girl?'

Clearly, he hadn't learnt a lesson in sensitivity from that debacle. Chetan seemed impressed by Sarkar's IIT pedigree and completely stupefied by my decision to quit an investment bank on Wall Street.

'But yaar, why? What do you ever hope to get from here?' he asked.

Hmm, where do I begin, I thought, and do I really know? I thought I knew yesterday when I was sharing a joint with a nameless software engineer who shared more of himself with me in a day than most of my colleagues back home shared with me over two years of working together. And I think I know, right now, sitting on this balcony with you perfect strangers who are so blasé about revealing everything about yourselves so easily to each other. I came here to live a real life once again, not an imitation of someone else's reality. Does that answer your question? I hope it does because I'm getting sick of answering it.

But I didn't reveal myself so easily. 'I don't know for sure, man. An international experience is valued in Wall Street. Global mergers and acquisitions, economic growth of developing markets and the expected retail explosion in India, all that kinda stuff, you know.' He didn't know. He seemed a trifle suspicious but let it fly.

Chetan's room was on my right and Sarkar's on the left. The two sides would go on to represent the two extreme ways that I would try to live my life at the IIM. Although I tended to lean towards Sarkar's self-destructive hedonistic philosophy, I developed more than a grudging respect for Chetan's unapologetic naked ambition for grades and jobs, however empty it seemed at most times.

We went to the cafeteria for lunch. The spread of authentic Indian food there reminded me of the platinum blonde who had found the sushi restaurant 'ethnic'. She would definitely climax at the food here. But then again, maybe not. This cafeteria wouldn't be ethnic enough for her. There were no photographs of the Taj Mahal on the walls, no Sanskrit calligraphy on the tablecloth and no intricate drawings of palaces on the plates. Just a whitewashed hall with rows of steel tables and foldable chairs. She would probably be disappointed.

The Bukhara Spice on Times Square with its sitar-wielding host was far more 'Indian'. Boy, was I glad I had got away!

Sitting there, devouring the best Indian meal I'd had in months, I felt almost optimistic at what lay ahead. There would be new faces and interesting experiences, and investment banking had set such a low base for happiness that it wouldn't be too difficult to cross that. I exchanged enthusiastic introductions with many of my new classmates over lunch that day. As Sarkar had predicted, most had heard of me and were suitably stupefied by my foolishness, and in one case, even annoyed by it.

'NRI, eh?' said a short, obese, angry-looking guy with spiked hair in a tone that could well have meant bastard or cocksucker.

'Not really,' I said. 'I'm not a non-resident Indian; I'm an American citizen.'

He shrugged. Same difference. 'What I don't understand is why you guys come back. Didn't you think about your roots or about your kids growing up in the American culture, or whatever it is that makes you return, when you left in the first place?' he asked.

There was a slight hush at the table. Even for India, where expressing offensive personal views was seemingly as common as asking, 'How was your weekend', he seemed to have crossed the line. Not that I could defend myself with any lofty assertions.

My coming here wasn't like Mahatma Gandhi returning from South Africa to lead India from darkness. Assisting India's development or anyone else's development for that matter was a distant concern in my mind. How could you save the world when you couldn't save yourself?

'And since when have you become a gatekeeper for India?' a calm voice asked him, saving me from the embarrassment of answering. It belonged to a tall, muscular, Mills-and-Boon sort of a guy with a short crew cut, who had been quietly eating his food so far. Like everyone else, he seemed to be in his early or mid-twenties, but his demeanour commanded respect.

'I'm just a concerned citizen,' the short dude said as if he had just smoked out a CIA agent hatching a plot against India.

'You should have been fighting with me in Kargil then,' the tall guy said. Ah-ha, I thought, an ex-army officer. 'Unless, of course, you were doing more important stuff for the country then. You must have been in politics, or in an NGO maybe?'

'No, I was working in a software firm,' the short guy said in a small voice.

'Canvassing for funds for war veterans in your spare time, perhaps?' the army officer said.

'I was busy preparing for the IIM entrance examination then,' he said, clearly embarrassed.

The table tittered with quiet laughter.

'Not everyone is born with a silver spoon,' he said, taking another dig at me before slinking away from the table.

Sarkar and I introduced ourselves to Vinod Singh, the army guy.

'Don't sweat it,' Vinod said. 'Everyone in India is an expert on nationalism. When we were fighting in Kashmir, we used to hear single-digit-IQ film personalities offer their view on military strategies on the radio.'

'Jingoism is an Indian problem,' said Sarkar caustically. 'Misplaced patriotism. Like our friend there.' He pointed to the vacant seat where the short, fat dude had sat. 'He would probably rate Navjot Singh Sidhu and Salman Khan as bigger patriots than Mahatma Gandhi or Nehru.'

Vinod's body shook with laughter. 'Sidhu is a cricketer and Khan is a movie star,' he explained to me. Then to Sarkar, 'They are heroes in their own right.'

'Heroes, my ass. Ask them to play for the country without wearing a Pepsi T-shirt and Dora underwear, then maybe I'll believe you. What's patriotic about being offered a million dollars in endorsements to play a dumb cricket match? It's a scam. See, that's why I want to get out of this country. It's like Toole's *Confederacy of Dunces*, idiots everywhere the eye can see,' said Sarkar. 'Yet our friend has come here,' he continued, pointing to me.

'Why did you leave the army?' I said quickly, trying to avert another discussion about my foolishness.

'The cafeteria is closing,' said Sarkar before Vinod could answer. 'Why don't we shift base to a dhaba?'

Lunches are long, elaborate affairs in India, and I hadn't realized we had been sitting there for a couple of hours. In my previous life, lunch took all of ten minutes as I grabbed a tuna sandwich every day at the same deli and wolfed it down in front of my computer while ferociously tracking the movement of our client company stocks. Now there were no more stocks to track, the market had closed down for me. Not that I was complaining.

'There is one right outside the campus,' said Sarkar. 'We can go on my bike.'

I had planned on going back to my room to do the suggested pre-read for the next day, our first day of classes, and Vinod also seemed a bit doubtful. Sensing our hesitation, Sarkar added, 'We'll be back soon, I promise. No drinking and stuff, just a cup of tea. I need a break.'

This was the first day and we didn't know then that Sarkar always needed a 'break'. Before we knew it, both of us had been convinced to ride pillion on Sarkar's bike through the mini-riot of Bangalore's streets.

We stopped at a highway stall, or dhaba as I learned to call it, a few miles away from campus, and sat down to enjoy a cup of tea. I smelled grass again.

After having studiously avoided drugs through high school and Yale, they seemed to be following me around ever since I had landed in India. It made me feel like the Alchemist—the universe seemed to be conspiring to fulfil my hidden desires.

Sarkar had lit up a joint and was smoking it openly while slurping his tea.

'Hey, aren't there any cops around here?' I asked, surprised by his brazenness.

He in turn seemed surprised by my ignorance. 'This is not America. There are bigger crimes for cops to bother about than arresting a poor student contemplating life over some gaanja. Here, you have one as well.'

The joint looked tempting. I reached out for it. It was stronger and harsher than the one I'd smoked yesterday.

We perched ourselves comfortably on the lone cot. Vinod casually placed his arm around Sarkar's shoulder. They looked like a gay version from the movie *Twins;* Sarkar was decidedly short and fat, and Vinod was way taller and built like an Adonis. I would have to get used to the Indian comfort with same-sex physical proximity, I thought. In another life, I would have thought Vinod and Sarkar were gay. Well, how did I know they weren't, I mused. I'd barely met them. But of course they weren't. They had revealed everything about themselves so quickly to me that matters of sexual preferences would definitely have come up. Both of them were similar in that way. They had the same self-assured air of 'Look, this is what I am. Don't like it? Then screw you. Go change yourself'.

I took a long drag and passed it on to Vinod, who refused. ('No gaanja for me. I have very few brain cells as it is.') He bought a bottle of rum from the dhaba and began emptying it steadily.

'You were saying? About leaving the army?' I asked again.

'Haan, yes,' Vinod said. 'I was very young, barely seventeen, when I joined the National Defence Academy, the Indian equivalent of your WestPoint, that is. All of us were dying to get into a war when we graduated. We couldn't believe our luck when the Kargil war was announced and we begged to be chosen for it.'

'Peace man. Peace out. No war,' said Sarkar sounding very stoned.

'Long story short, the war took its toll,' he said. 'We killed, they killed, some friends died, others lost their limbs, and we started to understand the politics of it for the first time. The old soldiers were all jaded as hell. It's useless, they said, as soon as we start driving the Pakistanis away, some politician will want Muslim votes and there will be peace again. War is useless, our biggest enemy is within us, they would say. Nothing made much sense and I didn't feel like a hero as I had thought I would. I just felt stupid,' said Vinod. 'But it wasn't that, really. It was…' He paused to drain his glass.

We stared at him expectantly.

'Well, nothing as such. I was reading a lot, newspapers, politics, war fiction, trying to make sense of things once I got back. When it came down to it, I realized, most of my work was pushing paper around, if I was lucky—and killing people if I wasn't. And then once… well, it sounds foolish…'

'Don't stop now,' said Sarkar, slouching on the cot and suddenly looking interested.

'No, nothing, it was just a stupid incident. My best mate, another lieutenant, had lost his leg in the war. His CO, commanding officer that is, was coming for a visit to the regiment and he was sent to make sure the CO's room was all right. So there he was, an officer in the army, a war hero who lost a leg for the country, standing on one leg and checking to ensure that the flush was working for the CO's visit. It was sad in a very pathetic sort of way. And I kind of decided that if I had to push paper and check the bathroom plumbing for a superior's visit, I'd rather do it in the corporate world. At least my family would get some money and security. It's kind of stupid, you know, how small things just set a chain of events in motion,' he said. He poured another glass for himself.

Barely a year older than me, and he had lived more than I would live in my whole life, I thought.

He was probably having a bayonet thrust at his stomach when I was eating sushi with Christine and trying to figure out how to recover my lost soul in India. The selfishness and insignificance of my crises was suddenly disconcerting.

'Good decision,' said Sarkar. 'Of course, you will miss out on the honour of Aishwarya Rai bringing a wreath to your funeral, and Annu Kapoor dedicating an episode of *Indian Idol* to your memory.'

Vinod broke into laughter. 'I didn't mean it that way. I respect the soldiers, I love my country, I don't ever want to leave India. But I was a misfit in the army, I think.'

'I think we are all perfect fits in business school, though,' said Sarkar, lazily cynical. 'We were all happy with our lives, and came here because we *really* wanted to get an MBA.'

It was such a pessimistic statement for the first day of business school that I couldn't help but laugh. He had given up even before starting; finally, I could tell Mom than I had met my match at running away from responsibility. I took another long drag of the joint.

The marijuana started to kick in and the world seemed to slow down a bit. The tea was excessively hot, milky and sweet—and tasted delicious. I could feel it slowly, pleasantly burning its way down my throat. The strong petrol fumes from passing vehicles started to smell inexplicably good. I could make out fine dust particles rising leisurely from the ground. The radio was playing soft, pleasing songs in an unknown, melodious language. The rays of the setting sun and the dust particles seemed to fuse together to create a radiant spectrum of colours. Funny, I thought, I couldn't seem to recall noticing dusk before. I felt a sudden burst of joy. Everything will work out, I said to myself, I just have to make the most of my time in India. However, I thought distractedly, looking at the joint in my hand, I need to be in my senses to do that. I shouldn't smoke up so much. I had smoked yesterday as well.

'We shouldn't do this, you know,' I said. My head felt heavy and I was struggling to form a coherent, complete thought.

'Do what?' Sarkar said.

'What?' I said, puzzled.

'You said we shouldn't do this,' he said.

'We shouldn't do what?' I asked.

'That's what I asked,' Sarkar said.

'No, I asked that,' I said, struggling to understand.

'No, you said we shouldn't do this,' Sarkar said.

'Do what?' I asked.

'What you said...' he said.

'What?' I said.

'You are stoned out of your minds. I can't listen to this conversation,' Vinod said unbearably loudly.

I sprawled on the cot, supporting my head with my right hand and holding the joint in my left, staring at the empty earthenware cups strewn on the ground.

Many peaceful, stoned hours passed. The dhaba began buzzing with night-time activity. Truck drivers with their cargo, large families on long journeys, random groups of college students on their dinner break—all arrived, made arbitrary conversation and left, each lost in their own world, trudging along, trying to make sense of the fundamental incomprehensibility that surrounded them every day. 'It's all a cosmic conspiracy,' the software engineer's words came back to me. I giggled at the recollection of the previous night.

A lazy, vacant eternity passed.

I saw Vinod get up to strike up a conversation with a group of soldiers who had just disembarked from their gigantic, oddly shaped green metallic monster of a vehicle. ('It's called a three-ton,' he told me. 'Why?' I asked. 'Because it weighs three tons, of course,' he said. 'But a car isn't called half-a-ton,' I said. 'I think I should go,' he said.)

Sarkar yawned lazily beside me.

Sarkar and Vinod were pretty cool, I thought, but could we ever become friends? Real friends, I mean. I had asked Baba once why all his friends were Indians.

'Dad, why don't you have a single close American friend?' I had asked somewhat tactlessly.

He was surprisingly forthright: 'There is always a

chasm between us, the divide caused by the absence of a common past. There are no shared memories of frat parties, tailgating, hazing and ball games that I can reminisce with them about, the same way they can't understand *Sholay* and Kapil Dev.'

Maybe he was right, I thought, and I'd never be able to get really close to my Indian friends. I had hardly caught any of the references—Annu whatever, some Sidhu. But it didn't seem to matter. Then again, maybe our generation was different. We had, after all, grown up in a flatter, more concordant world.

I turned to Sarkar. 'Do you think the absence of a common past matters, dude?' I asked.

He looked up drowsily, spewing blue smoke. 'Huh?' he said. 'What? Do you want to go back?'

'Go back where?' I asked.

'Back.' Sarkar sounded dazed.

'Okay, back,' I said.

'I can go, I guess, if you're tired,' he said.

'No, I'm fine. You decide if…' I said.

'No, *I'm* fine. You decide,' he said.

'No, I'm fine. You decide,' I replied, liking the sound of the words.

'No, I'm fine. *You* decide,' he said.

'No, I'm fine. You decide,' I said.

'Okay, I guess neither of us can make a decision,' he said.

Vinod came back just then and asked, 'Should we go back?'

Sarkar and I looked at each other and burst out laughing, nearly falling off the cot and rolling about uncontrollably. The hot ash from the joint fell on my forearms and the sudden burning sensation felt good.

'Let me ask again. Should we leave now? It's almost dawn and classes begin in a few hours. We've been sitting here for almost ten hours,' Vinod said.

I couldn't expend the effort to dissect the issue logically. Sarkar seemed lost in thought as well.

'Let's just go,' Vinod said. 'This is what happens when you smoke that gaanja of yours.'

Sarkar seemed to break from his trance at this comment and uttered his only coherent thought of the day.

'I smoke it in protest, man,' he said. 'Marijuana exists naturally as a plant. Who is the government to ban God's creation? It's like me wanting to make potatoes illegal because I don't like the way they taste.'

Wow, I thought, this sounds profound. What did he say again?

The chilly Bangalore air slowly knocked me back into my senses on the ride back. As we went back to our rooms, I was a trifle worried about the classes scheduled to begin in a few hours, as was Vinod, no doubt. Sarkar didn't seem to care one way or the other, and in fact suggested a final round back in our rooms, which both Vinod and I declined. I checked the time: 4:30 a.m. Classes began at eight in the morning. Of course, none of us had done any pre-work whatsoever. For the second day in a row, I had smoked up and barely slept, and though IIM seemed like a cool place so far, an assortment of unsolicited advisors had assured me that academics would be brutal and unmanageable. Lying on my bed stoned, this seemed incomprehensible. Whatever, I thought, as I drifted off to sleep.

I had seen worse before. How bad could this be?

4

How Bad Could This Be?

I could almost smell the testosterone when I entered the class the next day. I could see not more than five girls, and about sixty or seventy guys. Although no one else seemed remotely surprised by this, I found it astounding, given the global thrust for executive diversity.

The initial round of introductions also established that the lack of diversity wasn't limited to gender. Educational backgrounds were equally homogeneous. Almost all of the class comprised engineers from top technological institutes. A small minority had a background in finance and the remaining were from what could be termed diverse backgrounds—folks like Doctor Jatinder Pal, who had arrived on the honourable (some would say foolhardy) mission of providing unsolicited management acumen to the badly mismanaged world of public health in India. I knew this wasn't Harvard Business School, and I hadn't expected musicians, Olympic gold medallists or presidential speechwriters. However, I did find it ironic that an investment banker who would struggle to show how he was different in order to be considered for admission in a US business school, could end up becoming a poster boy for Indian B-School diversity.

Sarkar explained this phenomenon to me. 'Man, where do I begin? The whole system is completely screwed up. There are a billion people in this country, most of them right at the bottom of the food chain. Hence, there is no mass market for anything other than the basics, and certainly not for nobler pursuits like philosophy, literature, music or other fancy liberal arts kind of stuff. The only sure way to make a livelihood in India is to be in engineering or medicine, and while medicine requires a certain degree of patience and aptitude, being a software engineer in India requires neither. Look at me, for example. Despite being a computer engineering major, I have barely seen the computer lab at the IIT. India manages to churn out a million worthless engineers like me every year, and they all apply to business school to escape the futility of running backend computer operations for bloodsucking Americans.'

This was explained to me over a couple of cigarettes and chaar-pachchees (four and twenty-five, or four pieces of bread and twenty-five grams of butter) that we wolfed down between the orientation session and our first class of the day, managerial accounting.

My head ached from the seventy introductions we had heard during the orientation, Sarkar's incisive commentary on the sorry state of the Indian system and severe sleep deprivation. I planned to get some shut-eye in accounting class so I could be prepared for the marketing and statistics classes to follow. I was supremely confident of my accounting skills. After all, I had spent the last couple of years in the Mecca of the financial world. I was glad that it would be my first lecture after my two-year hiatus from school. It would help me ease back into academics.

The accounting professor turned out to be an attractive young woman with an animated face, black shoulder-length hair and alive, energetic eyes. Boy, I thought, the universe did seem to be conspiring to fulfil my dreams. My favourite subject, accounting; a beautiful professor; an Indian odyssey...

The professor didn't seem particularly interested in fraternizing with the students, though. She immediately launched into the lecture by explaining the harsh 'relative grading' system that she intended to follow in the course. There were four possible grades, A, B, C and D, that you could get, and these would be determined via a series of ten quizzes, a mid-semester exam and a final exam.

Simple enough. Although a couple of losers whined that twelve examinations over a three-month period seemed a bit of a stretch.

'But ma'am, that's almost an examination every week!'

Oh, these kids, I thought, it's just a quiz for heaven's sake! Go complain to your mothers.

I was impatient for the professor to get on with the real lecture so I could start establishing my academic domination in class. All my confusions aside, I had been an academic ace through high school and Yale, and I didn't expect this to be any different. I also figured that my class must have already stereotyped me as the dumb American and I was eager to make them eat crow. And of course, there was this whole matter of the star student and the cute professor.

But she wasn't done with the grading system yet. She explained that there were no absolute grades, all grading was relative and your performance depended on how the class performed. Only a few folks got an A, a majority got a B, some got a C and a few had to get a D or failing grade. This caused immediate dissent in class.

Someone spoke up. 'Ma'am, that seems unfair. Technically, even if I get 90 out of 100, I could still get a D because the rest of the class got a higher score. What are we trying to measure here? My ability to understand the subject or whether I can beat others in understanding the subject?'

The professor was quick with her response. 'What do you think success in corporate life is about? Your doing well or your doing better than your peers? My classes should simulate the reality you are going to face when you graduate from here, and my course is as much about learning accounting as it is about being the *best* at learning accounting.'

'Ma'am, do other professors have the same grading system?' This time the question was from my neighbour Chetan, who seemed particularly agitated that morning.

'Yes, some variation of it,' the professor said shortly. 'And let me answer the question you didn't ask. Some percentage of your class will not graduate from business school. It could be 10 per cent maximum, assuming the same folks get a D in every subject which is rare but has happened in the past, or it could be a lesser number, but there definitely will be a few who are left behind. But that is the nature of the game. It is not a reflection on you, it's just the way things are, and in a perverse sense, it's all for the best. Do I have to recount the clichés you all know so well: Albert Einstein failed his high school examinations, Bill Gates dropped out of Harvard, etc.? Maybe business school is not meant for you because there are bigger and better things awaiting you.'

There was a fresh note of panic on most faces now. At that point no one wanted anything bigger or better than graduating from school. I remained unperturbed. Relative grading was not an alien concept in the hypercompetitive world of Wall Street, and my academic concerns, if any, were more about being at the top of the class versus not being at the bottom.

'Any last questions before we move on to the real stuff?' The professor was now eager to begin the lesson. So was I. No hands.

'Okay. Let's start with the basics. Who can tell me what a balance sheet is?' she asked.

I raised my hand confidently. 'A balance sheet is a financial snapshot of a corporation which lists its assets, liabilities and shareholder equity at a fixed point in time,' I said.

That's it, I thought—suave, no rambling, no unnecessary information. I was the investment banker from Wall Street, after all, my time was money.

'Great answer,' beamed the professor, turning her pretty eyes towards me, 'I especially like the words "fixed point in time" since that is the difference between a balance sheet and an income statement.' The class looked awestruck.

I beamed back at her. I probably knew this stuff as well as she did, I thought. We definitely had a connection here. Maybe we could have a future together. We could live in one of those nice, spacious campus houses with a beautiful garden, have a couple of kids together, and I would teach at the IIM as well. But would it be all right if we both taught the same subject? Maybe I could…

'If you were forced to look at only one before making a decision to invest in a company, what would it be: a balance sheet or a profit-and-loss statement?' The professor interrupted my daydreams.

Uh-huh. No one asked *that* question on Wall Street. I used to work 100-hour weeks because we looked at everything. Why would we be forced to make a choice to look at just one? We had enough money to buy any financial document we wanted. Still, I could analyse the situation intellectually. Well, I would probably go with the income statement, but what about future cash flow estimation? Well, then, maybe a balance sheet...

'Great answer. Let's move on to financial ratios now,' I heard the professor say.

Someone had already answered the question. Hmm... I'll get the next question, I thought.

'What financial ratios would you look at in the balance sheet?' the professor asked.

Hey, this wasn't very structured! There was a certain method to financial analysis. You couldn't do it like this. Anyway, I would probably look at...

'Great answer.' The professor's voice rang in the background.

Again, someone had answered before I could process the question in my head.

'Let's move on to shareholder equity. What constitutes shareholder equity?' she asked.

Yep, I know that one. Let's see, when—

'Great answer,' I heard her tell someone yet again.

In that apocalyptic hour, which I would later think of as the turning point in my academic life, I lost all my confidence in accounting and pretty much everything related to business education. As she progressed further with the lesson and I fell progressively behind, my reactions changed from incomprehension to surprise to anger—at the superficiality of my knowledge and my inability to grasp even the most fundamental concepts she was talking about.

'Big deal,' I tried to console myself, 'none of this is practical anyway.'

I knew, though, that this wasn't true. Lectures like these were precisely the reason why Wall Street investment banking firms encouraged B-school. As Ruth, my boss, had said before I left, 'Most of it is going to be a waste of time but look out for the nuances. One small, extra insight that you bring back will be worth millions of dollars to the company someday.'

But today I wasn't getting any of those nuances as the professor sustained her blistering pace till the sixty-minute class finally screeched to a halt. She handed out the homework assignment for the next class: an analysis of seventeen intimidating financial exhibits, which constituted a consumer goods company's balance sheet.

'Two-page analysis, double-spaced, Microsoft Word, one-inch margin on all sides, Arial 12. Thought I would tell you so that all pages are created equal and I'm not looking through a magnifying glass to read someone's poetry. I promise I won't read after the second page, so go light on the prose and concentrate on the numbers,' she said as she walked out of class.

She didn't seem that sexy any longer. I didn't want to live with her in the campus housing or teach at the IIM or even study at the IIM any more.

I turned to Sarkar shakily. 'Let's get a quick cigarette fix before marketing begins. I'm fried.'

As we rushed to the cafeteria in the five-minute break before the marketing class, I said, 'Wow, man, that was something!' I was ready to launch into an account of my utter incomprehension at what just happened, fully expecting him to expand on the theme.

Instead, Sarkar said, 'Yep, man, wasn't it? What a woman, and pretty too! I had heard so much about how difficult accounting is, but this was so damn scientific and logical. Same story as the IITs— meaningless subjects made somewhat meaningful by the excellent faculty. I confess that I usually start off liking my studies before I begin to question their role in my larger turmoil-ridden world. Yet, this was fun.'

I looked at him, awestruck. 'Did you understand everything?' I asked, trying to mask the panic in my voice.

'Yep, I think so. I guess it's only because it was lesson one and she just covered the basics. But you must be mad at her. How dare she trivialize the noble world of financial statements with such simple explanations? Let it be,' he said, 'this stuff is trivial for an investment banker but for us engineering grads, it's good to get the hang of the fundamentals.'

I had learned my first lesson at B-school: never compare academic notes with an IITian even if he is your best friend and fellow stoner.

I wasn't the first American to reach that conclusion. Bill Gates had once famously said IIT = Harvard + MIT + Princeton. The phenomenon of the IITian was also familiar to me from Scott Adams's *Dilbert* which features Asok, the summer intern from IIT, who says in one strip, 'At the Indian Institute of Technology, I learned to use my huge brain but I try not to frighten ordinary people with any gratuitous displays of mental superiority.'

Sarkar's unwitting display of his intellectual prowess had frightened me, and he wasn't even supposed to be the most illustrious of the IITians. It was as if the more driven ones went to the US for higher studies, eventually becoming tech-billionaires in Silicon Valley, while the drifters went to the IIM and unwittingly dazzled the management sector with their sheer brain power.

It was a tough lesson to learn on my first day at B-school when I was struggling with my own apparent shortcomings. I walked back with him in silence as he continued to extol the virtues of the professor's teaching methods.

'You've suddenly become quiet, yaar. Things okay? I think you'll find the challenge you're looking for in marketing. By its nature, it is a pretty local field. I mean, marketing Diet Coke to an obese American who is dying of overeating should be inherently different from getting a starving Indian to replace one of his two meals a day with Coke,' Sarkar said.

I hadn't thought of that before, but now it gave me something else to worry about. If financial accounting, a subject that I knew in exactly the same form in the US, could be such a challenge, then the essentially local nature of disciplines such as marketing could well mean that I might be entering the elite 10 per cent club who didn't graduate from the IIM.

I am fucked, I thought. Absolutely, royally fucked. I had quit my job and travelled several thousand miles to flunk out of a course that didn't even really matter in the first place.

As it turned out, I survived marketing. The satisfying conversation Vinod and I had at the beginning of the class helped. ('Did you understand anything in accounting?' Vinod asked. 'Not after the first sentence on balance sheets,' I said. 'That's more than what I did. I didn't get past the grading system,' he said.) In fact, I was so engrossed in the marketing lecture that I didn't even notice Sarkar make an exit ten minutes before the scheduled end of the class. He didn't come back when the marketing lecture ended or even when the next class, advanced statistics for management, began.

'Has he gone back to his room in protest at having to attend classes?' whispered Vinod as the statistics professor walked in. I had no time to respond as the professor immediately launched into the intricacies of the course work.

It was Monday, 10:30 a.m., and whether it was the lack of sleep mixed with harsh Indian cigarettes or simply the superior Indian education system prevailing over an overused American banker's mind, statistics turned out to be another unmitigated disaster. I struggled to stay focused as the cherubic Bengali professor lectured about stuff that I vaguely remembered from another lifetime. However, just like accounting, the pace was far too intense for me to convert the vaguely familiar matter into anything clear. Just as I gave up pretending that I could figure anything out, Sarkar strolled into class nonchalantly—a full twenty minutes late.

'Today is the first class,' the professor said, interrupting the lecture to throw him an angry scowl, 'so I will let you in. But this won't do in the future. Now spare the apologies and take a seat so I can resume.'

Sarkar didn't seem particularly apologetic as he lazily walked up to the empty seat next to me. He reeked of marijuana. I stared at him in surprise.

'Are you crazy?' I whispered. 'Did you leave the marketing class to go smoke up? It's the first day of school for heaven's sake. I just don't believe you're doing this.'

'I couldn't tolerate that marketing nonsense, man. I went to get some pills actually, but ended up smoking an unfinished joint from yesterday,' he replied, showing me a vial packed with little white pills. I stared at his bloodshot eyes in disbelief as he washed down one with some water from the bottle on the desk. Just what's wrong with him, I thought.

Completely oblivious to my astonishment or the professor's steady drone, Sarkar began to draw in his notepad. Bored with scribbling down the comprehensible bits from the lecture after a while, I stole a glance at his doodling and was stunned once again. There, on the ordinary ruled page of his notepad, instead of a single word of what the professor had said was an elaborate sketch of Michelangelo's *The Fall of Man*—complete with the nudes, the tempting Satan and the avenging angel. He had taken all of ten minutes to create the replica. Unbelievable, I thought, shaking my head. Why was he wasting his time in business school?

And what about me, I thought, now completely distracted. Why was I in this classroom studying

correlation and regression equations when I had
no interest at all in doing an MBA—or doing just
about anything else for that matter? I hadn't come
here to 'get in touch with my roots' or understand
the 'duality of my identity' or any of the other
platitudes that second-generation immigrants
throw about weightily. Mom was right, I had run
away thinking that the farther I went, the deeper
the insight I would get into myself. What I hadn't
realized was that there probably wasn't a lot of
depth to peer into in the first place. It had been cool
to be decisive for a change and chuck everything,
now it felt foolishly impulsive. I looked around
the classroom—faces bent in concentration, brows
sweating, hands feverishly making notes; none
of them had been blessed with the opportunities
I had. Yet, I had walked away. How could I have
been so stupid?

'What is the real probability?'

When I looked up from my doodling next, the
professor was discussing some funny-sounding
probability theorem. He handed out a case study for
discussion. The central character, Chubby Charlie,
had to figure out whether the next cookie in a jar
of mixed cookies would be a chocolate chip cookie
or a butter almond one. Vinod caught my eye and
grinned. We were both thinking the same thing:
the cherubic statistics professor looked like Chubby
Charlie. He also seemed uncannily like someone

who would agonize over a cookie jar and get caught with his hands in one.

The professor asked the class to calculate the probability of Chubby Charlie getting another chocolate chip cookie. 'Why does Chubby Charlie think he has a 50 per cent chance when the probability is lower than that? What is his real probability?' he asked.

I could vaguely see the reapplication to the business world, but by then I was way beyond caring. I was sleepy and confused and just wanted the torture to end for the day.

'What is Chubby Charlie doing wrong?' The professor continued to push us.

'Is this a story from his repressed childhood?' I muttered to Sarkar, sitting comatose next to me. It wasn't even that funny, but he exploded into a sudden, stoned laughter.

The professor looked at him murderously. He already seemed to have made up his mind to dislike Sarkar since the time he had strolled into class twenty minutes late, looking every inch as stoned as he was.

'Seems like you have the answer,' he sneered at Sarkar.

'Not really, sir. Just got distracted a bit,' Sarkar mumbled, but the professor continued, 'Go on, you seem to be in a particularly jovial mood today. The question can't be that tough for you. What is the answer? Why is Chubby calculating the probability wrong?'

Sarkar screwed up his eyes for a minute, concentrating on the blackboard and said, 'Seems like Chubby isn't using the likelihood of prior events to predict future events and is basing them on just the current scenario. If he factors in the probabilities of the previous events, the overall probability of getting a chocolate-chip cookie would be closer to 45 per cent.'

Even the professor was surprised. 'That's pretty much it. Well stated. I couldn't have said it better myself,' he said shortly.

Sarkar's quick answer had caught me totally off guard. I could have sworn that like me, he was paying no attention at all. We had been winking and smiling for the past couple of minutes, sharing the Chubby Charlie joke with Vinod, and before that he had been making elaborate replicas of Michelangelo and God knows what else on his notepad. If I were asked the same question, I wouldn't have stumbled upon even a remotely sensible answer, except probably listing the different types of cookies available at the local Wal-Mart back home.

There is something inherently wrong with God's distribution of intelligence, I thought, if someone can walk into class twenty minutes late, pop a pill, smoke up, pay as little attention as possible and yet solve these godawful statistical problems without even batting an eyelid. I hope Sarkar is an exception, I said to myself, because if everyone in the class is like him, I had better start packing my bags.

The professor seemed a bit shaken by the episode too, or maybe he was just tired of droning on to a class of blank, tired faces.

'Let's break for now. No homework, but remember, the first statistics quiz will be two weeks from today.'

At 11:30 a.m., I took stock as classes formally ended for the day. It was brutal. Three lectures to revise, two of which I had barely understood, two case study analyses, the imminent threat of an accounting quiz and, finally, the sudden announcement of the mother of all quizzes—the dreaded statistics quiz: the first serious quiz at the IIM and the one which separated the men from the boys (given the proportion of women in the class, the chauvinistic term was justified). Legend had it that your performance in the first statistics quiz was eerily predictive of your rank in class at the end of two years. In some sense, this was logical since the symbolic value of acing the first quiz ensured that everyone had given their best to the quiz (almost everyone, that is—Sarkar chose not to waste precious smoking-up time preparing for such 'symbolic irrelevances').

As we walked back for lunch, I was determined to get my act together and focus on delivering my best in the quiz. Conquering the innate restlessness of the mind was what I had always been conditioned to do, whether in high school academics or the athletics squad at Yale, and I wasn't going to back down at the sign of some tough Indian competition. It was just a statistics quiz after all, hadn't I seen worse?

5

Just a Stats Quiz

I took to running every evening around the picturesque campus, revelling in the sensation of my feet pounding on the paved road, the throbbing pain in my calves and the reassuring river of sweat that drenched me. The sheer physical exhaustion of a six-mile run coupled with the usual sleep deprivation fused together to form a heady cocktail and I derived a perverse enjoyment in chasing my disorganized thoughts:

'Sarkar and Vinod are pretty cool. Glad I met them.'

But, 'No more male buddies. Try to get some action.'

Then, 'Should probably get connected with Nandini, she studied in the US as well, maybe I can get lucky there… But you don't even understand her questions in class, you dumb loser. What the hell will you talk about?'

And, 'Anyway, academically you are so miserably screwed dude, you have no right to think about anything else.'

Therefore: 'Maybe I should just stick to Sarkar and Vinod.'

And so it went till the run came to an end. While running had always been my mental release, here it evolved into a mystical, transcendental experience—an immediate antidote to the vague sense of impending doom that I hadn't been able to shake off since the time I landed in India.

But even the run failed to lift the wretched mood I was in the day before the statistics quiz.

I walked back to the hostel to be greeted by the usual half-puzzled, half-contemptuous 'Look at that American idiot, he has time to run! The stats quiz will teach him that this is not America' look from my hostel mates. But today, their frank bewilderment made me feel guilty instead of irritated. While the rest of the class buried their heads in books every waking moment, I spent almost two hours a day on such trivial pursuits as running and a post-run shower. I thought that running would help clear my head, but that didn't seem to be the case. Much to my frustration, I capitulated easily to the intellectually overdeveloped Indian brains all around me. I thought I was working hard, averaging four or five hours of sleep at night, but to my surprise I was unable to make a single inspired original comment in class. I soon understood why.

The short, spiky-haired dude, who had stopped just short of calling me a CIA operative during my first lunch at IIM, ran into me in the cafeteria the night before the quiz. Vikrant was fat, misshapen and delightfully transparent about his obsession with grades, ranks, internships, company recruitment talks and anything else that smelt even remotely of a way to a career. After disposing of the small talk ('Sorry for that day, I didn't mean it', 'By the way, what was your rank in Yale?', 'What was your CGPA?', 'How much did you get paid in Wall Street?', 'Do all bankers get to screw models?' etc.), he said he was feeling a bit sleepy that night.

'I haven't slept at all for the past two nights and have been averaging just about an hour or so for the last ten days. I think I'll turn in early tonight. I want to be fresh before the quiz,' he said.

It was 2:30 a.m. At best, he would manage five hours before the 8 a.m. quiz.

'You're kidding me, right? How can anyone survive on such little sleep?' I asked, already experiencing the familiar sinking sensation of knowing there would be another nasty Indian surprise in store.

'That's not really unusual here, is it? Most of the folks in my study group are doing the same,' he replied. 'And I used to follow the same schedule as a code coolie at Infosys pretty regularly. If I could keep those hours while writing software for a flush-valve manufacturer so they could supply screws for your loos in America on time, I can definitely keep them now before the first quiz in business school.'

I vowed to myself that I would immediately reduce my sleeping hours to compete effectively with these bastards. Thus I fell into the great Indian B-school trap of equating productivity with the number of hours spent awake. Soon, like everyone else, I would be benchmarking preparedness for examinations with sleeplessness: a quiz meant four hours of sleep, a midterm meant two hours and you were doomed if you got any sleep at all for the all-important end-term. Efficiency, prioritization and other such trifles became irrelevant. Later, I'd learn that the same principle was very much a part of Indian corporate culture: the number of hours you clocked in at office became a surrogate for how devoted you were to your job. Whether the time was spent in innumerable cigarette breaks or the occasional vada-pao interlude was irrelevant. You just needed to come early, stay late and neglect your family to wear Corporate India's badge of honour. Ironically, this went against everything you learned in B-school lectures on effective resource utilization, productivity drop with increased time spent on the job and negative impact of action versus result-based reward systems, etc. But then, when did business school claim to provide any vestige of a practical education?

After hearing about his 'study-group', I went to seek out my own—if you could call it that. I knocked on Sarkar's door to be greeted by the now familiar red eyes.

'Aao, Thakur, aao,' he said with a flourish. 'I had forgotten you live next to me. I haven't seen you at all for two weeks except in class. Are you okay, man?'

Sarkar himself looked quite well, sprawled on the bed in his smoky room. A glass of something dark, rum maybe, graced one hand and his statistics textbook the other. A joint lay in the ashtray and heavy metal played in the background. How the hell could anybody study this way?

'Yes, I'm fine, just very busy. Just came by to say hi. I have to solve the final tutorial sheet,' I replied.

'Arre yaar, always the American, never time to stop, never time to talk,' he said. 'I've looked at the tutorial sheets. I don't think you need to solve all the problems. Just look at a couple and you'll get the general sense. Feel free to ask me if you have any questions. I'm not an expert or anything, but I'm okay at mathematics and statistics kind of stuff.' He paused and took another long drag. 'None of this matters anyway.'

Sure, I thought, would you care to elaborate what else matters a day before the first quiz? But I didn't want to argue with him just then.

'Thanks for the offer, dude. I gotta go now. Let's catch up tomorrow after the exam,' I replied, thinking I had seen Goth-rocking stoned punks at Yale and I had seen brilliant analytical minds there, but I had never quite seen them both rolled into one.

I ran into Vinod on the way to my room. He was coming out of the phone booth, his giant frame dwarfing the small phone attendant, who looked almost scared collecting money from him.

'Calling home?' I asked. I had a sudden urge to call my parents and say that I was coming back.

'No,' Vinod replied quietly, unlike his usual cheerful self.

'Is everything okay? You don't sound too good,' I said.

'Well… not really. I was talking to a friend's mother. He was with me in Kashmir, didn't make it. It's been a year now, but I guess no amount of time will ever make things okay for her.'

I felt small worrying about statistics quizzes, business school, Manhattan, investment banking and so on. My existence affected no one's life other than my own. In another world—very close to mine—people died for their country and grieved for the families of their martyred friends.

Vinod seemed to read my thoughts. 'Anyway, forget all that. How is the preparation for the quiz coming along? I'm pretty worried about it,' he said.

I knew he didn't give a flying fuck about the stats quiz, the accounting case study or business school in general. He was just trying to be nice and regular, as if he wasn't any superior because he had stared death in the face and come back alive.

'Fine,' I said. 'How about yours?'

'I haven't done much, just looked at a sheet or two. Wasn't very interested, to be honest,' he said. 'Call me a rustic military clod, but I just can't believe managers need all this probability, random number generations and other complex statistics to make decisions in real life. It seems pretty useless.'

'Sarkar shares your views.' I smiled. 'He is a couple of steps ahead of you, though. He thinks everything is useless; the stats quiz, business school, life, everything.'

Vinod rolled his eyes and we both laughed. 'I've solved most of the tutorial sheets,' I said. 'Do you want some help?'

'Thanks a ton, man, but I'm good,' he said. He yawned. 'I'm going to head off to sleep. What time is the quiz?'

'First thing in the morning, 8:00 a.m,' I said ominously, expecting him to get flustered at the amount of work he still needed to get done.

'Oh,' he said, looking at his watch. 'I must have talked too long on the phone. I really must sleep now, can't do without my eight hours.'

Not a word about the quiz and the fact that he was so completely unprepared.

Inspired by his nonchalance, I went back to my room and decided to nap for a couple of hours before hitting the books again. I switched off the lights and tried to sleep to the soft strains of Pink Floyd escaping from Sarkar's room. But sleep eluded me.

Fleeting images of past happiness crossed my mind.
Simpler, uncomplicated times: hiking in the Grand
Canyon with Peter, Radha and Jeanne, my closest
friends from Yale; camping in Alaska, listening to
the heavy rumblings outside the tents, agonizing
whether we should stay quiet (Radha was sure it
was a grizzly bear) or shout (Peter was convinced
it was a black bear); their surprise when I revealed I
was going to India to 'search for myself'.

I felt wretched about my existence now. My
time in India hadn't helped me get any new insight
into myself. Instead, it had struck a serious blow at
the only things I hadn't been confused about: my
intellect and my ability. Stats problems jumbled
through my head—random distributions, normal
curves, probabilities—as I lay half-awake, half-
dreaming, trying desperately to stop. It became
worse: statistics mixed with accounting mixed with
Yale mixed with Wall Street mixed with surprised
friends mixed with angry parents mixed with Vinod
fighting off a soldier with a bayonet. I finally gave
up all attempts to sleep. This was criminal, I thought,
two hours wasted just trying to sleep, and now I felt
even more exhausted.

I went to wash my face to begin on the statistics
tutorials again and caught a glimpse of myself in the
bathroom mirror. Puffy eyes, sunken face. Just what
was I doing here, I thought. I smiled. It seemed
almost comic. I had come ten thousand miles to

study the intricacies of how business gets done in India. And how exactly was this supposed to help me when I went back to Manhattan? I would probably be at an interview for a job at the bank again where some interviewer would look at me quizzically and ask the same question that everyone was asking me, 'And why exactly did you go to India?'

I would finally lose it then, I guess, and tell him what I really thought.

'Because I'm stupid,' I would say. 'But that's okay. You don't need Einstein to analyse the revenue streams of our underwear client. I'll do just fine.'

I cheered up at the thought of giving that answer and made my way to the examination hall.

Eight a.m. Tense, anxious moments as the quiz was handed out. An immediate rush to act as folks started scratching their pens against the paper without fully processing the question. I did the same. Busily doing something sustained the illusion that I was solving the questions. I finished two of the three questions very quickly, confident that I had got them right. If the stats quiz is supposed to be the indicator of how one ends up academically at the IIM, I thought, with a sudden burst of confidence, watch out as the dumb American strides to the top.

Several things happened as I read the third question. From the corner of my eye, I saw a classmate suddenly convulse in his seat. He seemed to be having some sort of a seizure—white foam and the works, like Sanjeev Kumar in one of Mom's old Bollywood movies. Some of us rushed to his seat, wanting to help but not knowing how to as he continued to writhe on the floor. Within seconds, Dr Pal, the medical doctor in our class, came running from the opposite end of the hall and took control of the situation. Very soon, with an efficiency that would make 911 proud, the institute ambulance came to take him to the emergency room. Order was restored.

As we were returning to our seats, I realized that apart from the few of us who had been distracted enough to get up, the others had kept working through this entire episode as if nothing unusual had happened.

There were many times, this being one of them, when I almost envied my colleagues for their single-minded pursuit of grades and careers. Their goals were concrete and stationary, not moving targets like mine. This clarity made them happy, at least temporarily, as they crossed milestone after milestone, racing towards the finish line of the rainbow that never ended. Not that I was any superior, heck, I didn't even know what my undefined loftier ambitions were. I was just an overfed, confused American searching for his soul—the biggest cliché in the world.

'Don't reach for the secret too soon.' Peter's words came to mind as I tried to concentrate on the test again, and focused on finishing the third and final question. Whether a result of the distractions I had just experienced or the final sputtering of my tired brain, I struggled and struggled, unable to solve it as the minutes ticked by. I approached it from every possible angle, creating elaborate decision-trees for each of Chubby Charlie's possible decisions, but there seemed to be some essential piece of data I was missing. A perfect score and resultant deliverance from everyday self-doubt seemed tantalizingly close, but remained unattainable. Two minutes left, another false lead and I abandoned the question to recheck my answers to the others. One minute left and I discovered a calculation error in my answer to the second question. With a silent cry of despair, I started to fix it as the ruthlessly efficient exam coordinator snatched the paper from my hand. Damn, I thought, frustrated with myself, I came so close to acing this but choked at the last minute.

I walked out of the exam hall feeling morose when Sarkar and Vinod descended upon me.

'Ah, finally our elusive friend. You pulled off the ultimate disappearing act in the last two weeks. So, did you ace the quiz?' asked Vinod.

'Balls, dude, I blew it at the last minute. Did you manage to get the third question?' I asked.

Vinod was nonchalant as usual. 'Kahaan, boss? Didn't even get to it. I barely managed to finish the second question, actually. But chill. It's just a quiz.'

'What about you?' I asked Sarkar, eager to be reassured that we were all in the same boat, sinking fast.

Sarkar didn't answer the question. 'Let's skip the autopsy, guys. It's almost noon, half the day has already been wasted. Hey Vinod, what say I give our American friend a real Indian education today?' He winked.

'I think he's getting more of it than he needs already,' said Vinod.

'The real management lessons of India aren't in the classrooms,' said Sarkar melodramatically. 'You have to meet the dealers and the pimps, self-made entrepreneurs who are single-handedly fighting the system to provide high-value goods to discerning customers. So valued are their services that they don't find customers, customers find them. That bastard, Kotler, should have taken some lessons from them instead of from corrupt cola giants.'

'Cut the crap, will you?' I said. 'I'm in. Where do we go?' Anything to forget the mess I had made of the quiz.

'Vinod, do you mind getting the booze while I take him for a glimpse of enlightenment?' Sarkar said.

'Only if you promise to shut up when you are back,' Vinod said.

I followed Sarkar to his bike. 'Okay, so we need to score gaanja from somewhere,' he said, rubbing his hands. There was a wild glint in his eyes. 'My usual supplier is the dhobi, the washerman that is, but that bastard went off on a holiday without informing me. I finished off the stash yesterday before the quiz. So where should we get it from? Now, let's approach this problem analytically, like a B-school case study.'

I couldn't tell if he was serious. 'Dude, are you sure? You are new to Bangalore too, and I don't want to get into any trouble with the police and stuff. I've got enough to deal with already.'

'Hop on, firang, this is India. Where there is money, there is a way,' he replied and we set off on his bike towards the city.

Unwittingly, I was mentored in the fine art of searching for banned substances in India that day. 'Okay, here is Rule Number One: always start in areas surrounding bus stations and taxi stands,' Sarkar shouted above the din of the traffic. 'Bus and taxi drivers are notorious dope users.'

'Why them?' I asked. 'In India especially, I thought it would be the addiction of the rich.'

'Hardly. Taxi drivers dope out of necessity rather than for recreation,' he replied. 'Supply-demand economics. Driving a bus or a taxi is quite a coveted job in India. You get a decent salary, take your family out for free rides, sometimes even make money from tips—when your client is a foreigner and not an Indian, that is. Indians don't give tips. Entry barriers are low. You don't need to clear any examination to get your driving license. Just get your photo taken, pay a small bribe and you get a brand-new license in a matter of minutes. As a result, hundreds of unemployed young men want to become bus or taxi drivers every year, a situation that all the vehicle owners exploit.'

As we entered the deafening chaos of Majestic bus station, I was convinced we would die or kill someone as Sarkar swerved the bike dangerously to avoid hitting the billion people on the narrow streets. 'Why don't you concentrate on the road for a while? We can talk later,' I said.

'Ha, ha! Don't worry, firang, we'll survive. There is a method in this madness that you will understand soon. Anyway, I was saying, these vehicle owners, they drive their drivers hard, pardon the pun. A Toyota Qualis driver we knew in IIT had once been on the road continuously for almost two months from Delhi to Benares, Lucknow, Rajasthan, Manali, to every place imaginable in north India, with barely two to three hours of sleep every night. How do you unwind from the stress of driving in this inhuman traffic and get ready for the next journey in the two hours you are given to rest? You turn to pills and gaanja, a quick, efficient rejuvenating kick minus the sluggishness and hangover that cheap booze causes.'

More shouts and screams in Kannada. We had finally arrived at the bus stand. Music blared from bus stereos, passengers crowded around cigarette and tea stalls, carelessly spitting chewed pan on the road and on each other, bus conductors screamed their destinations, banging the sides of buses, and engines revved up or shuddered to death all around us.

Sarkar parked the bike next to a tea stall and asked the owner, a short, potbellied man with a fierce moustache, 'Boss, koi jugaad hai?'

As the owner stared nonplussed, Sarkar started speaking to me again: 'Rule Number Two: Never ask for the stuff directly, lest someone lets loose a cop on you. Of course, the cop won't put you in jail or anything, but then he becomes another person in the food chain you need to pay. There is a universal language which works here.'

He was right. 'Koi jugaad hai' or 'any fixes' seemed illogical and harmless to the uninitiated, but was somehow clear to the supplier. The fourth guy he asked, an auto-rickshaw driver, responded in Hindi, 'Hai na, saab. I have everything. What do you want?'

The conversation moved carefully forward as both avoided stating what was being sought to ensure their tracks were covered.

'What do you have?' asked Sarkar.

'Everything, I told you. The question is not how much water I have, the question is how much can you drink?' replied the wizened old driver philosophically. He sounds like a Zen monk rather than a drug dealer, I thought.

More Zen followed.

'The kind of water I want to drink is forbidden by the law,' said Sarkar cryptically.

'Water that is too pure has no fish,' said the driver. 'The government can outlaw the water but can anyone ban the thirst? The thirsty will find their own pond.'

They went on for a while until the driver finally said, 'Saab, Nepali hai, Tibet ki hai, gori hai, schoolgirl, housewife, lawyer, doctor, you tell.' As would happen many times in these hunts, he had assumed that we were seeking women. It did establish though that he was a fellow corrupt soul, so Sarkar proceeded with his demands. 'No, we don't want all that. Can you get us some gaanja?'

'Haan, saab, definitely. Very high-quality stuff. I have used it myself, though I don't use it any more,' said the driver. 'While you're trying to escape, I'm trying to return,' he added mournfully.

They haggled for a while, settling at the princely sum of Rs 750 (fifteen dollars) for a kilo, and we jumped into his auto.

He started driving us through small, narrow streets lined with filth from the overflowing drains, with stray dogs snapping at the auto and an overpowering stench of rotten waste. Despite the bright day, everything seemed dark and foreboding in the dirty squalor of these narrow alleys. I didn't like this. A month ago, I was a high-flying banker with a promising future. Today I found myself being driven along stinking drains teeming with rats. How had I missed the romance in this transformation?

Before long, our man stopped outside one of the rundown houses and got out wordlessly.

'Aren't you worried?' I asked Sarkar, desperately wanting to be reassured. 'You've already given him the money and he knows you have more. He could do anything now. People are killed for way less in India.'

'Final lesson for the day,' he replied, clearly enjoying my discomfort. 'Yeh bharose ka dhanda hai. This is a trade of trust. Do you kill the hen that lays golden eggs? He knows I'm an addict and will keep coming back again. You tell me, if his stuff is good and reasonably priced, would you go about chasing someone in Bangalore like this to get it the next time? Chill, he'll be back with excellent stuff. I can't wait to smell it.'

Irrefutable logic. And I was now a certified expert in the important art of buying marijuana in India. My parents would be proud back home in Louisville, Kentucky.

As Sarkar had promised, the auto-rickshaw driver came back with the stuff rolled up in a newspaper. He then drove us back to the bus stand, smiling slyly as he handed over the bag.

'A tip, perhaps? You couldn't have got the message without the messenger,' he said.

Zen again.

We knew he had taken a significant cut from the money Sarkar had given him, but he was asking for a tip as was expected of him. I was in a generous mood, relieved and happy to get out, and gave the driver-cum-dealer-cum-Zen monk a hundred-rupee note without even a token protest.

'Arre, you rich American, this is what you do after all the time I spent bargaining?' Sarkar said as we walked off.

We raced through the city to make our way back to campus for an evening of debauchery in Sarkar's room. Hesitant as I was to admit it to myself, I had enjoyed the thrill of the marijuana chase and had all but forgotten about the debacle of the statistics quiz earlier that day. Vinod was already in the room, steadily working his way through a bottle of the local poison, Old Monk, and singing along with the stereo. He didn't stop singing when we entered the room. I liked him for being comfortable enough to drink and sing alone.

Sarkar lit up our first joint of the day.

'Let's chase it,' Sarkar said, and he taught me the fine art of 'chasing', taking a quick drag of an ordinary cigarette before inhaling the smoke from the joint. Round and round it went, with cries of 'chase, chase, chase', until we'd had several rounds between us (even as Vinod continued to abstain).

'Do you know what happened to Ravindra

today?' I asked, suddenly reminded of his convulsing, writhing body in the examination hall.

'Yeah, I found out,' Vinod said. 'He is in intensive care right now. Apparently, he suffered from a severe epileptic attack because he hasn't been taking his medicines regularly since he came here. Time constraints, I guess, and the fact that your whole schedule goes so completely awry here.'

'Jesus, thank God it was just an epileptic attack,' I replied. 'I thought it was something serious like a heart attack or something. This place could easily do that to you.'

Sarkar laughed. 'You heartless bastard, thanking God for an epileptic attack.'

The dope was just starting to hit when there was a sudden knock on the door.

'Did you hear that?' I asked Sarkar over the loud strains of some noisy metal number in the background.

He was standing next to the door. 'Yeah, give me a sec,' he said and opened it, looking perfectly sober. He did not attempt to hide anything, I noted. Smoking grass seemed acceptable here; it seemed as common a recreation activity as, say, watching porn in high school. You didn't really make a public display of it, but you didn't hide it either.

'Could you turn down the music a bit? People live next door in case you forgot.' It was Chetan, looking pretty pissed off.

'Chetan, my man, come on in. We are celebrating the end of the stats quiz. We got some grass especially for you. We'll smoke one together to toast you sticking it to the Man,' Sarkar said mockingly.

'No thanks, some other time. My study group is coming here for the economics case study discussion, but I guess we will go somewhere else. You guys have fun,' Chetan replied, his anger somewhat dissipated by Sarkar's unexpected response. As usual, he wasn't perceptive enough to catch the irony in Sarkar's invitation.

Sarkar closed the door behind him. He echoed the same fleeting thought that I'd had during the statistics quiz that morning: 'Sometimes, I admire the simplicity of Chetan's complications. All he lives for is the next quiz, the next case study and the next grade point average. Bastard, there is not a cry of anguish from him about anything deeper than being two minutes late for a project submission deadline,' he said.

'Well,' I began hesitatingly, 'I can't claim to be any different. For the past couple of weeks I've been the same—obsessing about my inability to understand basic accounting concepts, struggling with sleep before the stats quiz because I want so badly to do well and trying to make a mark by asking a brilliant question in class. It's like being back in tenth grade and trying to please my dad with my SAT scores. I came here to get some insights about myself, but all I've managed to do is unearth even more demons.'

The dope seemed to be a real downer today. It was making me think of all sorts of things that I didn't want to think about. Was my sometime success at school in the US based only on the fact that real competition was elsewhere? Why was I here? Why was I anywhere, for that matter? And finally, the mother of all questions—what exactly was the nature of existence and why were there always more questions than answers?

I realized I had asked the last question aloud. Sarkar dragged on his joint and drawled, 'Samrat boy, your problem is that you think too much. Just accept that there are no answers anywhere, man; it's the nature of existence. Hmmm… do you want to know my take on that?'

I didn't really, but there would be no stopping him now, I knew. Sarkar sounded just like Peter did when he was stoned. Peter would walk into my room, baked as a cake, and lecture me for hours on religion and philosophy and remember just about nothing the next day. There is no difference between people when you get into the real heart of things, I thought. American, Indian, everyone was essentially the same when it really came down to it. But life is so much about the superficialities that differences always appear starker than the similarities. Gosh, I thought, that stuff we're smoking must be strong. I sounded like one of those 'The World is a Family' tree-hugging, planet-saving bastards.

'Where are you lost, man?' Sarkar asked. He was itching to hear himself talk. 'I was talking about the nature of existence. Well, think of the smooth, even circumference of… of say, this book.' He picked up our marketing textbook, which looked brand new, probably because he had never bothered to open it. 'Now, imagine the surfaces of hundreds, millions, billions of such books stacked together. What do you get? A never-ending plane that just goes on and on, no beginning, no end, just flowing, it just *is*. That is what existence is. Me, you, everyone—we are mere specks on the surface who just come and go, the plane exists as it always did. Captain Ahab realized it too late; the sea rolls on as it has for a thousand years.'

Infinite planes and Captain Ahab—I felt even more confused than before. Which of my questions was he answering? He just liked the sound of his own voice, I concluded. Vinod seemed to agree.

'Didn't I tell you to stop talking nonsense when you came back?' he said. He screwed up his nose and flapped his hand in front of his nose. 'I survived the war, now I'm going to die of second-hand smoke. What's up with you, smoking like a Himalayan hippie? Aren't there more tasteful ways to kill yourself?'

'None as satisfying. The whole cycle is fundamentally wretched; the unknown vacuum inside us can never be filled,' said Sarkar. 'Doom is inevitable, so I embrace it. I enjoy this… this slow, deliberate destruction. Kind of like a moth slowly flirting with the flame instead of being surprised when it's thrust in by an unknown force. It gives some meaning to life.'

'Maybe you should smoke less,' said Vinod. 'Life will appear less hazy then.'

Sarkar extended the joint to him. 'Try it sometime. Everyone needs to puff the magic dragon once. It gives a whole new dimension to things.'

'Sure thing,' said Vinod sweetly. 'This is next on my list, after trying the herbal supplement which promises me an extra five inches, giving my internet banking password to the Nigerian who wants to transfer $50 million into my bank account and applying the cream that's going to "give my bomb a longer timer".'

'Oh damn.' I got up with a start. 'I have to meet someone for a coffee date. Hell, I think I'm late already.' I'd been reminded of the date by the 'extra five inches' and the 'male-enhancing cream' comments, which made me feel vaguely ashamed.

'Who?' said Sarkar and Vinod together.

'A girl,' I said. 'I gotta rush now.'

'Are you gonna let us know or should we follow you?' Sarkar said.

'Don't follow me. She is a happy camper, I don't want to depress her,' I said.

'Very funny. It's Nandini, isn't it?' said Sarkar. 'She is my classmate from IIT. I know what kind of guys she likes.'

'I am neither confirming nor denying your hypothesis,' I said, mimicking the statistics professor.

Vinod whistled. 'She's cute—and tall, too. I should take some tips from you.'

Sarkar was grinning from ear to ear. 'Why are you smiling, you bastard?' I asked.

'Nothing,' he said.

'What?' said Vinod.

He drew an imaginary circle in the air. 'This is a circle,' he said. He drew a line in between. 'This is the diameter.'

I looked at him quizzically.

'You're at opposite ends of the diameter; she's gonna break your balls,' he said soothingly.

'Opposites attract,' I said.

He laughed. 'Let's see about that. We'll be waiting here when you get back.'

'Don't count on it. I might not be back tonight,' I said as I walked out of the room.

I hurried to the cafeteria, our meeting place, my head a bit cloudy from the grass. I stepped into the bathroom outside the cafeteria and washed my face. I looked terrible. Grimy, puffy, red-eyed, stale-smelling breath—I wondered what she saw in me. Technically, she hadn't asked me out, but she had dropped as many hints as possible. Or at least used the Business School version of pick-up lines. ('I studied in Philadelphia in the eighth grade,' she had said, 'I would love to hear your perspective on the differences in the education system between the US and India over coffee some day.') Very sexy.

Nandini was waiting in the cafeteria.

'Sorry, sorry, sorry,' I said. 'I lost track of time.'

She *was* tall. She must have been at least 5'10", barely a few inches shorter than I was, pleasantly slim, medium-length light brown hair and a determined though kindly look on her face. Smiling, she extended her hand.

'No worries at all.' She smiled awkwardly, brushing her hair back with her free hand.

Now it struck me why she had seemed vaguely familiar. She reminded me of Dominique from *Fountainhead*, the wet dream of all the misfits in the world.

'It's a miracle you came at all, given that you hang out with Shine Sarkar.' She smiled.

I laughed. 'You know him well?'

'We were classmates at IIT,' she said. 'Technically, that is. He would rarely grace us with his presence in class, though. But he was famous, notorious, rather.'

'I can imagine,' I said.

'What about you? Were you a good student at school?' she said.

'Just about average,' I said.

'Come on, don't be modest,' she said. 'Someone said you were a valedictorian at Yale.'

Rumours like these made me appear even more foolish than I was. I wasn't just letting myself down, I was letting the entire American education system down. I felt proud of this momentous accomplishment.

'Are you enjoying school?' I said, changing the subject.

'Oh yes,' she said, her face lighting up. 'Business school is so much more interesting than engineering. I find everything fascinating. Economics, marketing, finance, organizational behaviour, it's all new to me. But you must have had a lot of exposure to all this in banking, right?'

Uh-huh, another touchy subject.

'A little bit,' I said. 'Are you planning to go into banking after this?'

'No, no,' she said. 'Management consulting.'

Another 100-hour-a-week job that rivalled banking in its soullessness. 'Why?' I asked.

'My goal is to be a CEO of a Fortune 100 corporation. Management consulting helps you get there fastest. After five years of consulting at Mckinsey, I want to move into an internal strategy role at a large firm. Two or three years of that, and I will be given operating responsibility, the fast-track path to becoming the CEO,' she said.

'Okay,' I said. I was beginning to float as the marijuana began to hit me again. I tried to get a grip on myself.

'What about you?' she asked. Her voice seemed to come from far away.

'What about me?' I said.

'Are you going to join a bank after school?' she said.

'I don't know,' I said.

'There are so many different subjects in B-school. It takes some time to figure out your real passion,' she said.

'Yes,' I said. With the way I was going, I thought, I'd be lucky to find a passion on my death bed.

'What about your long-term plans?' she said.

'Long-term plans?' I repeated dumbly.

'I mean, would you rather be a CEO of a large corporation or run your own business?' she said.

There was never going to be a second date, I knew. The only people I attracted or get attracted to were misfits and oddballs, and she was neither. I gave up trying to concentrate and let the weed kick in.

'Neither,' I said.

A few more 'no', 'neither' and 'I don't know' about my future plans followed.

She frowned and said something. By now, I was too toasted to understand what she said, but I liked the way her scowl reached her eyes. She had a frantic, rushed air about her, as if there were a million places she wanted to be in simultaneously. She spoke again.

'What?' I said, trying to look away from her eyebrows. She looked at me impatiently.

'I said, what do you want to be?'

I was silent for a moment. 'A writer,' I said. This was the first time the thought had entered my mind, but I quite liked it. 'Or maybe a film-maker.' Which sounded even cooler.

She frowned again. 'Shouldn't you be in film school or a creative arts school or something then?'

'You're right,' I said. 'This conversation has been really helpful. I'm going to seriously think things through now.'

I could feel the laughter rise within me. I was about as serious about joining film school as I was about being in business school in India—which wasn't saying much.

She looked at me as if she didn't trust me.

'So, what are your hobbies?' she said.

'I like reading,' I said. Which was true. 'Business books, management literature, etc.' I was being mean, I knew. And didn't want to be. It was an irrational act of rebellion against a world where everyone seemed to know exactly where they were going. Except for me and my buddies, that is.

I missed them, all of a sudden.

'It was a pleasure to meet you. Good luck with the course,' I said.

She left after saying a terse goodbye. I started to feel bad for behaving like an asshole, but immediately forgave myself. She'll be a CEO one day, I told myself, while you'll still be a mid-level manager pushing paper in some godforsaken organization and cracking bad jokes to yourself.

I glided to Sarkar's room.

'... nonsense, you're just a privileged SOB,' Vinod was saying to Sarkar as I entered the room. He turned around.

'Ah hah! Welcome back,' said Vinod. 'Aren't you back a little early? I am glad you came, though. The Buddha here was talking about suffering being the nature of the human spirit and how happiness lies in its acceptance. I'm tearing up at the nobility of this great soul and how much he is suffering. Just look at him.'

Sarkar was sitting as I had left him—head leaning against the music system, one hand on his temple, a joint in the other hand. He smiled lazily.

'So did she approve your five-year plan and your ten-year plan? Are you preparing a report on your vision, mission and goals for your next date?' he said.

'Bastard,' I said. 'You should've warned me beforehand.'

'You said opposites attract,' he said. 'And I wanted to give true love a chance.'

Vinod guffawed. 'If God made you Cupid, I would swear off love.'

I leaned against the wall. From the quiz in the morning to the hunt for weed to the stoned date with Nandini, it had been an exhausting day. The sound of the guitar reverberated against the walls and the drums seemed to thunder away at the bottom of the room. An irregularity on the adjoining bright whitewashed wall distracted me. I peered harder: a nail. Probably the last occupant of the room had used it to put up a poster or a photograph. Sarkar's walls were bare. No photographs, no posters, no memories. It occurred to me that he never talked about his family or childhood. I continued to stare at the nail, wondering disconnectedly why a blatant extrovert like Sarkar was so quiet about his personal life. But I was too much at peace to ask him.

Sarkar and Vinod seemed to have fallen silent as well. Perhaps that was all there was to it, I thought: a joint, good music, friends with whom you could be as comfortable in silence as in conversation, a desire to be in no other moment but the one you were in. It wasn't all that complicated. Maybe *this* was my long-term plan.

Vinod and I finally made our way out of Sarkar's room at dawn. Sarkar whined as usual at seeing the party break up.

'Stay a while, guys. Let's have breakfast before we go to sleep,' he said. 'Seriously, what do we have to worry about? Soon we'll have large multinational corporations throwing big fat bones at us so that we become their loyal dogs for life. Really, whether we have ten-year plans like Nandini or not, it isn't as if getting a job is a matter of life or death for us.'

6

Getting a Job Is a Matter of Life or Death

Soon, I settled into a life of unhappy mediocrity. The results of the statistics quiz came back. I had scored a nine out of fifteen, falling somewhere in the centre of the batch. It was true after all, what they said about the stats quiz: it became an indicator of my future performance at the institute. Multiple quizzes across a range of subjects cemented my position as a consistent mediocre performer with little deviation on the plus or minus side.

I guess it would have been fine if, like Vinod, I was broadly contented with my lot, happy about exploring new areas of study and accepting that my colleagues were better suited to perform in this situation. Vinod had made six out of fifteen in the quiz and was firmly in the bottom quartile of the class, but it didn't seem to bother him too much. Examinations, according to him, were a necessary evil en route to a broader awareness of the world via the B-school curriculum. He was fine to just be here. But that was Vinod, and this was me. I was so driven by a need to achieve and be respected for my achievements—whether they mattered to me or not—that I felt acutely depressed at being just another student trudging with my books to the classroom, a face in the sea of faces around me.

Every day, I struggled with the same questions. 'Why am I here? What truth am I discovering, closeted in this campus twenty-four hours a day? Didn't I see more of India in the US via the regular dose of Mom's Bollywood movies and Indian magazines? Why am I sitting in India reading management books written by American authors? God, let me just graduate quickly and end this torture. Do I even need to graduate—why can't I just leave now?'

To nobody's surprise and everyone's envy, Sarkar became one of two students to get a perfect score in the statistics quiz and he continued his astonishing run in almost every other subject except organizational behaviour. OB became Sarkar's bête noire as he struggled with the pretentious essay-type questions. His strained relations with the subject deteriorated further when he submitted a two-line assignment that begged for reams and reams of paper. It was our end-term project: 'Describe three incidents in your life that gave you a deeper insight into yourself and shaped your personal leadership values.'

The class went berserk inventing glorious incidents of profound enlightenment and many trees were felled in the heroic quest for getting a good grade in this pointless assignment. Sarkar wrote what everyone wanted to write: 'My leadership values are constantly evolving. I'm unsure whether I should define them at this stage without taking on more serious leadership responsibilities.'

Period. No incidents, no explanations.

The professor was convinced he was being mocked, and Sarkar's final grade in the course turned out to be a D. But then, like Vinod, he genuinely didn't care.

Nonetheless, but for OB, Sarkar was unstoppable and ruled in every other subject including 'softer courses' such as marketing and managerial communication. Life isn't meant to be fair, and our class arrived at that harsh realization when a pill-popping, chain-smoking, alcohol-abusing, marijuana addict effortlessly rose to the top of the class even as the rest of us spent night after sleepless night hanging on, just trying to survive.

In direct, almost poetic contrast, the other person to score perfect marks in the statistics quiz was my other neighbour, Chetan. He was blatantly, unapologetically chasing grades, and remained under constant duress as he saw Sarkar snapping at his heels for the Presidential Gold Medal awarded to the top ranker of the class. It was almost comical to see the tense, always-on-the-edge Chetan chasing the nonchalant Sarkar after every quiz to benchmark his scores. Chetan lived in a state of perpetual anxiety—the anxiety of falling behind someone in a quiz, of not getting the highest-paying job on campus, of losing the Presidential Gold Medal. For me, he symbolized the paradox of how one requires almost no 'management' skills to be the best manager at the best B-school in India. I could safely say that Chetan had no desire to ever 'manage' or 'develop' anyone else's potential save his own. Even in that, he was so insecure about his abilities that he was phenomenally indecisive, agonizing to death over the smallest decisions. ('I can't decide whether the footnotes in each page should be font size eight or nine. Nine looks better but will the professor cut marks for using an odd-numbered font size?' he said in one of our project group meetings.) However, his indecisiveness, poor communication skills and unabashed self-promotion did little to prevent him from becoming the lead runner for the Best Manager of the Batch medal.

Better Chetan than me, I thought one particularly frustrating day, as I struggled with a statistics problem due for electronic submission in less than ten minutes. I was in the computer lab at 1:50 a.m. and, as usual, I was countering sleep with multiple cups of strong tea and cigarettes, fighting the urge to rush to Sarkar for help once again.

'Damn it,' I said aloud, ready to quit, when Chetan himself slid in next to me. 'Can I help you with that? I just finished mine an hour ago,' he said.

Hmm, that's weird, I thought. I'd been here two months and Chetan hadn't bothered to acknowledge my existence after our lunch together the first day.

Should I sell my soul for a five per cent quiz? I briefly contemplated refusing him, but didn't pursue that line of thinking. I was learning slowly that stopping oneself from thinking too hard was one of the best qualities a manager could acquire.

'Yes, thanks a ton. I was struggling with how to calculate the variance of a random distribution. I don't seem to recall the professor talking about it in class,' I said.

Quickly, Chetan showed me how to use some obscure toolbar options in the statistical software, fill in some imposing Greek-looking variables in an open dialog box and pressed the Run button to submit the analyses.

'Thanks, dude, I owe you one.' I let out a sigh of relief as the ticker hit 2 a.m. and I got the confirmation that I had submitted the assignment in time.

'Glad I could help. Do you want to grab some tea?' he responded unexpectedly. I looked at him curiously, trying to guess the reason for this chumminess. Chetan, like most of the class, was conducting transactions in business school— you give me something, I'll give you something in return—and wasn't seeking any meaningful emotional attachment, love, friendship or memories from the institute. Gordon Gekko in *Wall Street* would have been proud to mentor him. Chetan symbolized what Gekko stood for: 'If you need a friend, get a dog, kiddo… It's all about the bucks, kid. The rest is conversation.'

Why then the need for this conversation? As far as I could see, I had nothing whatsoever to offer in this transaction. I was the beacon of mediocrity, and shone not in a single class or assignment. I tried to recall if I had done anything exceptional lately and realized with shame that I couldn't think of anything since I had come to India.

Chetan revealed his intentions over tea. 'Have you started preparing for summer placements yet?' he asked. Summer placement season or the crazy three-day company recruitment process for summer internships was supposed to begin in a month, a fact that had completely slipped my mind. A month seemed several lifetimes away. But I wasn't about to reveal the sorry state of my affairs to Chetan. I said, 'I've started to create some plans and schedules.' In reality, the brief moments I had spent thinking of summer placements were all in the context of returning to the illusion of happiness I had created in Manhattan. I had a standing offer from my ex-employer in Wall Street and was sorely tempted to go back and pick up the fragments of my old life.

'Well, I wanted to ask you,' Chetan went on, smiling like a Catholic priest about to stick it into an altar boy, 'if you would like to join our placement preparation group—Jain and Nitin and me, that is.' The other two names he had just mentioned were the top-rankers in the class, rarely seen, seldom heard, always buried up to their arse in books.

Chetan continued, 'We could really benefit from your experience in investment banking.' Now it was starting to make sense. 'And,' he hesitated, 'your contacts in the banking industry.' Oh, Chetan, you pathetic bastard, couldn't you have done this with a little more finesse? I should have guessed. My supposed contacts in investment banking would soon make me a hot property in the batch and Chetan, as usual, had figured it out quicker than anyone else.

'Thanks for your offer, man. I'm honoured, of course, but I guess I'll just plod along on my own,' I told him. 'I don't want to drag you guys down since I don't know what my schedule is going to be. I'm more a solitary preparation kinda guy anyway.'

Even if I wanted to ace summer placements, I couldn't see myself closeted for hours in Chetan's room discussing interview questions with his insufferable crew. He looked somewhat surprised and very disappointed. He hadn't expected that answer, especially since he had just dropped Jain's name. Jain had become something of a legend after his perfect score in a recent brutal economics quiz in which half the class had failed to get a single mark.

Chetan's interjection did force me to start thinking seriously about summer placements and despite it being about 3 a.m., I decided to sort things out in my head by going for a run. Unlike American schools, which have a steady progression of companies coming to recruit on campus over several months, Indian B-schools have an illogically intense three-day window where more than a hundred companies arrive to recruit from a class of 200-odd students. To ensure most people get their pick, company visits are slotted in this period based on student preferences. The first day of recruiting, enigmatically titled Day Zero, features all the top-ticket investment banking and consulting companies since these usually pay the most lucrative salaries and offer foreign postings—clearly the most important factors in luring B-School students (who cares about minutiae like job satisfaction?). The next day's top slots go to top global consumer goods companies followed by hot regional-banking jobs with IT companies making up the rear. The following day goes to second-notch companies in these sectors. The final day is reserved for public sector and government companies because serving the Government of India is firmly in the backseat for salary-hungry students in the (government-subsidized) IIM.

The system works well for the top-rankers as they are given several job offers before they pick one on Day Zero. An average student, however, goes through approximately 25-30 stressful interviews and is rejected by several companies in the space of a couple of days before finally landing a job. Which merely exhausts you. What kills you is when you are among the bottom-rung folks who have to go through as many as 70-80 interviews in three torturous days, and correspondingly as many rejections, before getting a job.

Even that is still okay, I guess, an essential, traumatic B-school experience that becomes a distant memory as the years go by. The worst off are those who are left without a job at the end of the process and are slowly, painfully absorbed over the next couple of months via the random act of a company seeking a last-minute candidate to fill a gap. Their spirit is completely broken by then. After being openly rejected for a dumb corporate internship almost a hundred times, only the toughest manage to hold on to any illusion of self-worth.

And then there are the mumbled discussions of fellow students—'He hasn't got a job yet!' —in hallways to contend with, sometimes real, sometimes imagined. 'B-school kills many an innocent mockingbird,' Sarkar used to say, and the first ones to break completely are the summer placement rejects. As we were to discover, failure in summer placements coupled with the crushing feeling of shabby academic performance could often have hazardous consequences.

'I'm not afraid of summer placements. Interviews have always been my strength,' I told myself. 'Well, so was academics until now.'

'But interviews are different.'

'Oh, really, what is different about them?'

'Well, go back then! The whole class wants to get into investment banking and you already have an offer from the best bank.'

I started my run that night with the familiar havoc in my head.

Maybe it was the absolute solitude of the 3 a.m. run or the haunted, eerie desolation of the beautiful campus, but I did end up arriving at a decision by the end of the run. Although, I thought ironically, it was a decision arrived at by elimination rather than selection. I wasn't going back to Manhattan for my internship, I decided. I had come here in search of something, however abstract, and I wasn't going to take the soft option so early in the game. Was my search more personal than professional? I didn't know, so with a numerical flourish that would make Chubby Charlie proud, I decided to give both equal probability and eliminated all foreign jobs and local banking jobs from my consideration.

IT companies were out of the question, of course. Even in the US, at the height of the Indian technology outsourcing boom, I had been dreadful at computers. I was routinely embarrassed by the white computer administrator in the investment bank who would stare confounded at me when I called him with alarming frequency to fix my computer issues.

'What is the world coming to? How can an Indian ask an American to fix his computer?' would be the unasked question in his eyes.

'You stereotyping bastard, it's because I'm an American investment banker like everyone around here. This isn't my skill set,' was my unspoken answer.

Anyhow, this left only India-based management consulting and marketing jobs, and I decided to go after them wholeheartedly. I felt good about my decision and almost looked forward to the perverse randomness of consulting the manager of a sugar factory plant somewhere in rural Uttar Pradesh. He would likely have hair growing out of his ears and would be surprised by my complete lack of knowledge about manufacturing, silently wondering why his useless bosses sitting in Mumbai had found the need to hire a bozo with a thick American accent to help with a broken supply chain in Uttar Pradesh. Best of luck, bastards, here I come, I thought, suddenly exhilarated. I felt good again—the silent agony of indecision no longer troubled me.

What is it about running and me, I thought,

returning to my hostel room. Every time I came back from a run, all my problems seemed to dissolve in the rivulets of sweat that poured down my back.

I saw a light in Sarkar's room and decided to see if he had anything I could smoke up in celebration. Vinod was already there and I felt a momentary pang when I saw the easy familiarity that had developed between them over the past two months. I had been so possessed by my own insecurities that barring a spare weekend or two, I had hardly spent any time with them. I felt small and selfish. They were always there when I needed someone to unwind with, but I virtually ignored them otherwise. So wrapped up was I in my desire to succeed in my little world that I had forgotten to define success. Would I be happy if, hypothetically, I managed to ace the course? Probably not, since I had done so consistently in Yale, yet my only truly happy memories of the place were of the time spent with Peter and Radha, of long discussions over coffee and cigarettes and staring out into the hazy, uncertain future together. A weird contradiction—the absence of academic, or for that matter, all material achievement made me unhappy, but its presence made me no happier. Ah, the elusive nature of happiness, I thought, entering the room, noticing immediately that both of them looked very sober. In fact, to my surprise, the characteristically laidback pair was discussing summer placements as well.

'Window of opportunity daab do bhai,' Sarkar was saying animatedly as I entered, 'Just grab the window of opportunity, this is not a time for confusion.'

❋

Apparently, Vinod was going through the same turmoil as I was—should one go for investment-banking, consulting, marketing, human resources or IT, and how does one make the decision after just two months of being swamped with an overload of unfamiliar information in B-school?

Sarkar's unasked for advice was whimsical and erratic as usual. 'Yaar, here is my logic. All these decisions are as simple as deciding where to vacation. Should you go to tourist spots, say Paris or Rome, where everyone goes, for example? You will immediately cringe and cry out no, behenchod, my vacation has to be different. I can't end up clicking a photograph on a gondola in Venice like Chikli *Bua* and show it to disinterested relatives over chicken tikkas in the living room. But here is my perspective. Hypothetically, if this was your honeymoon or an occasion that is unlikely to come again, what would you do? Would you go to an unknown, unpredictable location like the Amazon rainforest, or would you find safety in numbers and sip coffee in a café in Paris, knowing you couldn't possibly go wrong with that? Placements are similar. It is a once-in-a-lifetime opportunity. Just follow the tried-and-tested path. If everyone thinks investment-banking jobs are hot, just go for them. How wrong can you go with that? That's what I've always done. No clue what to do with life? Take the IIT exam because 500,000 people take it every year. No clue what to do after IIT? Take the IIM exam because 300,000 people apply for the IIM. Simple, man. Never over-think.'

Vinod was laughing. 'You have a gift for all this pseudo-philosophical bullshit. And you haven't been helpful at all, by the way.'

He turned to me. 'Samrat... wow! You went for a run? Big game. I love this shit, boss. I've become a wuss since I came here. Let's run together tomorrow. So, what's your plan for placements?'

I told them my strategy. They were suitably impressed. 'That is stupendous clarity from the most confused soul among us,' said Sarkar.

'Most confused? Who, me?' I whined.

'Why not?' Sarkar countered. 'In the thirty-year history of the institute, no one has seen a banker from Wall Street come here to get his MBA, and I'm sure that in the next hundred years, no one will. And while that doesn't surprise me—I would probably have done something similar—I'm surprised by your manic attention to academics and grades. I mean, I would have expected you to be doping around reading the Gita or the Upanishads, searching for the meaning of life, and yet I barely see you at all because you are busy studying for a petty five per cent weighted statistics quiz.'

Vinod jumped in as well. 'It is a bit confounding. What exactly are you going to get out of grades anyway? You already have an open offer from the company that all the top rankers want to get into.'

'I don't know, okay?' I said irritably. 'Who defined this confusion scale anyway? I find it equally confusing that a guy who could be using his mind to do something meaningful is trying to stop himself from thinking by smoking up and popping pills.'

Vinod agreed. 'I think we're all fucked. We have no right to define degrees of confusion.' Sensing my irritation, he changed the subject. 'Can either of you actually imagine working in a corporation and being paid for it? It sounds pretty remote. I mean, I did work in the army, but it was all fun and games, like an extension of the National Defence Academy—versus a real job. It's difficult to imagine coming to work every day in a suit and tie, running Excel files, attending strategy meetings and such.'

'You get used to it,' I said shortly.

That's how I had felt as well when I was about to graduate from Yale. Working for a living hadn't seemed possible, but when it did happen, it seemed natural. Or did it? I had never quite settled down at work and on most days, everything had seemed like such a waste. All the talk about beating competition, serving your clients, creating value for shareholders and making a difference to client companies had always sounded hollow, make-believe and unreal. 'At least stop pretending it matters, please. What difference does it make to the cosmos if the client company's stock price rises by a dime? Who really gives a fuck?' I had wanted to say so many times to my chronically overenthusiastic colleagues at the bank.

'I think there are certain kinds of people who're cut out to work their balls off at work every day and feel fulfilled,' Sarkar said. 'For one, it has to be someone who doesn't think too much because—'

'Let's analyse all this once we get a job,' Vinod cut off Sarkar before he launched into his usual monologue about the futility of the cycle of life: getting a job, marriage, kids, death. 'Let's make a pact, okay? Let's study together seriously for the next month, get a job and then discuss all this. I, for one, have no fall-back plans. If it isn't a job here, I will be back to checking bathrooms for an army general's visit. Let's hold on to the life- and system-bashing discussions until summer placements are over.'

*

In the following month, not only the three of us, but the whole class became obsessed with placements even as the onslaught of incomprehensible lectures, surprise quizzes and intense case study discussions continued unabated. It was a pressure cauldron. Various incidents of petty politics started coming to light. Chetan had taken Nandini's case study analysis from the printer and read it before class to poke holes in her presentation in class; Jain had not communicated a message from the professor to the class so that he had the edge before a quiz; Hari, in charge of the tutorial sheets, had 'forgotten' to keep a professor's assignment at the library Xerox counter a day before the exams; someone had forwarded Manik's e-mail, in which he had called a lecturer an 'old hag', to the lecturer in question from an unknown e-mail account. Such mindless incidents became commonplace.

In the meantime, summer placement preparations began in full earnest. Resumes were sexed up with make-believe incidents of past glory (the winner of a skipping rope competition in first grade called himself an 'accomplished track and field athlete'), mock interviews were held, agonizing, painstaking research on companies was completed. Everyone had done enough preparation to convince one set of interviewers that analysing spreadsheets in the credit card division of a local bank was their life's passion, and in the same breath make an impassioned plea to another set of interviewers about how they'd always had wet dreams about selling toothpaste in rural India. Why this charade, I thought. Aren't the interviewers business school graduates too? Haven't they experienced the complete lack of direction that one feels in the first few months here? But that's how the game was played, so that's how we played it.

Sarkar, Vinod and I began to gather in my room every night to prepare for interviews. I gave Vinod and Sarkar a snapshot into investment banking interviews.

'Always, always boast unabashedly and show naked, hungry ambition,' I advised them. 'A brilliant guy from Yale got rejected because he said he only wanted 50,000 dollars in his bank after five years. I said I wanted at least a million. I was lying, of course. All I wanted was to be happy, but banking interviews are not the place to discuss trivial emotions like happiness.'

We laboriously filled the long forms that marketing companies thrust on us.

'Should I write about my skills in procuring a certain substance that day?' Sarkar agonized in mock seriousness over a consumer goods company's essay-type question: Give an example where you set a vision, successfully overcame obstacles and collaborated with multiple stakeholders to achieve that vision. 'I think it is a great example of setting a simple vision—get some grass, somehow, anyhow, collaborating with multiple stakeholders—three chai-wallahs and two auto-rickshaw guys, while successfully overcoming obstacles—the auto-wallah turned out to be a bloody pimp and wanted to get us women instead of weed!'

He continued to rant: 'Seriously, what are you supposed to write? All eight questions are asking the same thing in different ways. Listen to the next one: "Give an example of a time when you demonstrated leadership by aligning your team to deliver an important result." Bastards. How is "setting a vision" different from "leadership" or "aligning your team" different from "collaboration"? I'm going crazy with this nonsense. If this is what marketing is about, at least one field is eliminated from my consideration.'

Sarkar's final marketing forms were laughable in their honesty. In answer to a particular question, for example, he wrote, 'See Question 2. Same answer.'

Vinod, on the other hand, probably delivered the strongest answers without realizing it. For a typical question like 'Give an example of a situation where you demonstrated significant risk-taking behaviour', while the rest of us wrote about the extreme risk of changing the word 'happy' to 'glad' five minutes before a project submission deadline, Vinod's answer was, 'Three soldiers in the eight-member sniper team I led in the Kargil war were killed by enemy fire. Instead of following conventional wisdom and staying together as a group, I split the team into three groups… and finally managed to kill the entire enemy battalion.'

And I had thought my incident about picking up a penny stock and making a million for my investment bank was risk-taking at its very best!

The three-day placement season began with a vengeance. It was like a carnival, only a stressful one. At any given time during the three days, there were at least fifty companies and their stuffy executives ('Will we become assholes like them one day?' asked Sarkar) on campus, and the buzz of about a hundred students being interviewed simultaneously. The students most in demand were being shuttled between rooms and had to shift gears in seconds from peddling detergents to peddling automobile insurance. The pace of activity was dizzying as job offers were made every second and people either accepted, happy that it was all over, or accepted before rushing for the next interview to negotiate a slightly higher salary or the elusive foreign posting.

The companies on Day Zero were all international banking and consulting firms and I hadn't applied for any. Relaxed—probably the only guy on campus to be in that happy state—I strolled down in my loafers and shorts to check on Sarkar, Vinod and a couple of others. But 'strolling' was impossible. I found myself being sucked into a thousand different tasks—consoling Nandini who burst into tears after being rejected by both Goldman Sachs and Deutsche Bank in the space of ten minutes ('It's all for the good,' I told her—and this time, I wasn't lying), fetching forgotten coats and ties, giving last-minute advice on cracking soulless banking interviews. As I rushed to grab lunch for Chetan, I realized with satisfaction that everyone chipped in when it really mattered. This was placements, not a five per cent stats quiz. It was important and we were all in it together, petty grievances against each other forgotten. Everyone wanted to ace the placements, but no one really wanted anyone else to get screwed in the process.

Exhausted from running around, I went out for a cigarette break at the tea stall and ran into another classmate, Kunal. He had piqued my curiosity on the first day because he had majored in zoology—a monstrous abnormality in the heavily engineer-dominated class. But things being what they were, I had barely exchanged a word with him in the first few months of being on campus. He looked a bit low, so I decided to make small talk with him.

'No interviews today, huh?' I enquired, already guessing the answer.

His tall, lean frame drooped a bit, and he rubbed his red eyes. 'Nope, neither today, nor tomorrow actually. No one on Day Zero or Day One shortlisted me. My first interview begins only mid-Day Two with a software company I have no interest in, but I guess I don't have a choice. I just want this to end—get the first job I can and get out of this place for good,' he replied, a surprisingly long answer to my polite question.

The dude must be lonely, I thought.

'Don't take it too hard, man. It's not like it's final placements, it's just an internship,' I said. I felt bad for him. I liked his quiet, soft-spoken demeanour in class but had hardly had a chance to know him better.

'I'm not sure things are going to be any different then,' he replied. 'It's a vicious cycle: unconventional background = bad internship = bad final placement, if any at all. But I was prepared for this when I came here. I knew that the only way to break the equation was to get good grades here. I thought I could manage that easily, since I have always been a topper. Out here, though, I'm struggling, struggling bad. I am right at the bottom of the class in everything, even in organizational behaviour, which I should be doing well at as a psychology minor. Life is careening out of control… can't handle things, can't sleep nights, I keep feeling humiliated at my terrible performance in quizzes, and now this internship fiasco. I'm truly fucked. Back home in Ranchi, things were different, you know. I was a state gold medallist, a tennis champion, and now I'm a miserable nobody. Do you understand what I'm saying?'

Don't I understand, kid? Welcome to my world. While you were being awarded your gold medal in Ranchi, I was being sucked off by the best investment banks on Wall Street. How the mighty fall.

I tried to cheer him up with an optimism I didn't feel. 'I'm no different, man, no interviews lined up for today, and I'm struggling with academics as well. Barring a few folks, I think everybody is going through the same thing, some more than others. Just relax, take it easy. It's hard enough to get into IIM without setting unreasonable expectations for oneself. Think of all your friends outside who'd give an arm and a leg to be in your position today.'

I was hardly a credible source for dispensing advice. Can the shipwrecked save the drowning?

Chetan walked by then for a quick cigarette fix between interviews, said hi to me but barely glanced at Kunal. He finished his cigarette and left. It triggered something in Kunal and all of a sudden he turned angry.

'You don't understand. Everyone has issues, but they all have some redeeming quality that makes them different. In your case, it is your investment-banking background or your American accent or your going around in Bermudas or your Bob Marley T-Shirt or whatever—you're special, you're different. I have nothing, NOTHING that makes me stand out.' He was almost shouting now. 'And that's why people act as if I don't exist, as if I'm a piece of furniture or something. Look at Chetan, he didn't even acknowledge me.'

I thought he was overreacting; everyone knew that Chetan was an unsocial bastard. But I let it be.

He came close to me and I smelt alcohol on his breath. 'Anyway, I'm leaving now, thanks for listening. Best of luck for the placements, I hope you get what you want.' He walked off abruptly.

This can't be good, I thought, you don't get drunk on Day Zero even if you aren't shortlisted for interviews. I guess Kunal's isolation and subsequent humiliation had increased manifold on seeing his colleagues dressed up in black suits and fancy ties, ready to be interviewed by the best companies of the world. Two months ago, he must have aspired to get into these companies, but he had probably realized the futility of his ambitions. I vowed to stop wallowing in self-pity and start being more sensitive to people around me. I was sure that I behaved like Chetan without knowing or meaning to. I thought of walking back with Kunal and grabbing lunch or something, but decided against it. I'll talk to him after placements, I thought, and went back to the main building to see whether Sarkar had managed to reach the final round of Deutsche Bank, London.

*

Three days later, Kunal killed himself. As a final act of defiance against an uncaring world, he decided to be different in death, and didn't select the textbook method of suspending himself from the ceiling fan with a rope. We found out later that he had electrocuted himself by making a scientific circuit between his body, the wire cable and the electrical switch in his room. He had probably thought that this gave him an option until the very end. He would have time to think while carefully constructing the circuit and could decide not to pull the switch. But then, he had probably realized that his past visions of glory would soon be replaced by a life of hopeless mediocrity. He had chosen the ultimate release and pulled the switch.

Could I have stopped it from happening if I had followed him that day? Probably not, although I felt guilty as hell for not doing anything despite seeing him cry out for help. But a lot had happened in those three days, and I was reasonably certain that a shoulder to cry on, on Day Zero, would not have helped Kunal get over the rejections of seventy companies between Day Two and the end of Day Three. The whole system was at fault, I tried to rationalize, and I could hardly have corrected the problem by myself.

Neither was the problem uniquely Indian, I thought on my daily run. In every top institution in the world, the burden of unreasonable expectations takes lives. We keep striving for bigger and bigger goals until we forget what we are striving for. Why else would a banker with a net worth of fifty million dollars work one hundred-hour weeks and risk a breakdown to generate his next ten million-dollar bonus? In India, the phenomenon is probably exacerbated because kids, particularly sons, are the unparalleled centre of their parents' existence. The son enters this inhuman pressure cauldron of overachievers and is surprised to see that the world doesn't care about him as much as his mother does. His lonely mind starts creating its own private hell. If he's lucky, he'll survive, get a decent job, find a nice Indian wife who worships him like his mother did, and slowly forget these confused, tormented years. But if he isn't, he'll become one of the few odd suicides that are recorded every year at the IITs and IIMs.

Vinod had a different prognosis. 'Loneliness, boss, that's what it is,' he told me. 'It fucks you up. An officer in my barracks in Jodhpur also killed himself. Can you believe that? A soldier who almost died in the war defending himself and others from enemy attacks every minute of the day for weeks on end, came back to peaceful, quiet little Jodhpur, and one day, boom! He shoots himself in the head, just like that. He lived in the next room and I was the first to see him. It was ghastly. Have you ever seen anyone's brains come out of their head?'

I shook my head, fascinated as usual by his stories.

'Well, you don't want to. Blood was splattered all over the walls. It seemed like such a waste that I remember feeling angry rather than sorry. I wanted to shake him up and tell him, "For God's sake, couldn't you have just walked up to my room and talked about what was going on in your head? I have nightmares, too, about all that we did during the war. Even I feel that it was all in vain." Man, I wish I could have told Kunal to just get out there, make some real friends and talk to people. It doesn't get simpler than that.'

I couldn't help smiling when he completed his story. The good Dr Vinod, with no medical training but many strong opinions, had just dismissed the entire Post Traumatic Stress Disorder industry in the US in a flash with his able diagnosis.

Easily explained or not, Kunal's suicide did shake us up and for a while we couldn't stop talking about it. Vinod, Sarkar and I had been successful in our placements, but our petty triumphs seemed meaningless. Not surprisingly, Sarkar had landed a banking internship in London, one of the plum jobs going. I knew he would be exceptionally good as a trader with his decisiveness and devil-may-care attitude. Whether he wanted to do well or not was an entirely different question, and one even he probably didn't have an answer to.

Vinod had landed a top consulting job despite his utter disdain for big management consultancy theories (he passionately hated 'big picture', 'value creation', '7E theory', 2x2 matrices and assorted consultancy jargon). They must have been impressed by his refreshing candour and obvious leadership abilities because his academic credentials were way below the norm.

I had accepted an offer from Shivam Chemicals, among the best brand management jobs on campus, while rejecting one from McCarthy Consulting, a decision that was to make me an even bigger enigma to the batch. McCarthy Consulting was one of the most coveted jobs that season, given its hot salaries and supposedly glamorous job profile. Money be damned, I had thought, I just didn't like the ultra-competitive, hyper-aggressive people who came to interview. It was as if they were obliged to act rude and arrogant, because the Man sitting in New York had prescribed that all hotshot consultants behave that way. If I had to live with this nonsense every day, I thought, I might as well earn a better salary on Wall Street, where being obnoxious is a badge of honour that the best bankers wear proudly. Not that I knew what to expect at Shivam Chemicals, but I was looking forward to my internship peddling soaps and shampoos in some obscure small town in the hinterlands. I had a vague sense that something important was going to happen to me there.

I kept thinking about the unfairness of it all—I had made career choices for frivolous reasons while the person sitting next to me in class had committed suicide because he didn't even get to a point where he could exercise a choice. Why were our destinies so different? Who decides a privileged birth for one and an endless struggle for another? Is there anything like free will or is everything predetermined? Is there really a point to existence or are we just pawns in a larger, incomprehensible game?

7

The Larger,
Incomprehensible Game

The excitement behind summer placements was over, and so was the shock of the first suicide in the batch. Kunal's death, although disturbing, wasn't completely unexpected. I think almost everyone had had that question at the back of his or her mind: 'Who would be the first to break?'

So, in a cruel, perverse way, his suicide was almost a relief. Some of us realized that our struggles were not unique and, though it wasn't apparent, people around us were suffering even more than we were. Others realized how thin the line was between being extremely stressed and caving in, and that slowed them down fractionally. The knowledge of shared misery had a redemptive quality and for a while, people were nicer, less competitive and more trustful of each other. But like every event that happens to someone else, Kunal's suicide also became stale news, and soon some of the fundamental questions that the incident raised were forgotten in the whirlwind of academic activity that surrounded us—quizzes, midterms, end terms, group projects. Grades, once again, triumphed over mundane matters like life and death.

Sarkar seemed profoundly shaken by the incident, though. He walked into my room late one night, just before the end of the first semester. We had a ten-day break coming up before the second semester began.

'Samrat, boy,' he said, 'have you thought of what you plan to do in the break?'

'Not really,' I said, 'going back home is not an option since it's too small a break. I guess I just want to catch up on my sleep for the first couple of days, and then I'll probably go hiking in Coorg or Ooty. Nothing definite yet.'

I hadn't made a concrete plan, but I knew that I desperately needed sleep and large breaths of cold mountain air. I also knew that both Vinod and Sarkar would invite me to their respective homes for the break, but I had no desire to go. I was exhausted and couldn't bear the thought of staying with a large Indian family who would likely overwhelm me with their generosity.

'Sounds good. But I was just thinking that maybe you might… might want to accompany me,' Sarkar said, sounding unusually hesitant. 'I'm planning to go for this ten-day meditation course to Dharamsala in the foothills of the Himalayas. It is kind of like a… like a spiritual retreat. No, that sounds terribly phoney. It is more like a scientific course to help you get a taste of salvation or nirvana or liberation or whatever you call it. Shit, that sounds worse!'

He seemed genuinely uncomfortable now, and I was enjoying his rare discomfiture.

Hmm… intriguing, both the course and Sarkar's embarrassed admission that he was being pulled into the great Indian spiritual racket.

'Scientific nirvana? Sounds like a scam. Can't believe you fell for it, dude. How much do we pay for this scheme? Is it like a Colgate teeth whitening advertisement—enlightenment in ten days or your money back?' I replied, attempting to add to his suffering. But Sarkar was back in his element with the question.

'See, that's the most incredible part. No fee. What's more, even lodging and meals are completely free, which you can imagine is no mean achievement in India. There is this big Indian industrialist, Mr S.N. Goenka, who pays for the course out of his own pocket and the meagre donations he collects. He practises Buddha's meditation techniques and is convinced that you can embark on the path to nirvana by practising those. He actively propagates the meditation as his service to humanity.' Sarkar paused. 'See, I know you think this is the great Indian spiritual crap. I thought the same way. But I have heard him speak once. He's the real deal, not your levitating, walking-on-the-water "tap your spiritual potential by giving me a blowjob" kind of phoney sadhu. I've seen my share of spiritual bastards and I'm convinced this one won't be getting sucked off by underage girls while preaching abstinence.'

I remained cynical. The last thing I wanted to turn into was a pot-smoking American hippie in the Himalayas. But I was too exhausted to prolong the discussion by refusing to participate in Sarkar's plans.

'Sounds interesting. Count me in,' I said. It couldn't hurt much anyway. I didn't have a plan, and the foothills of the Himalayas seemed as good a place as any to loaf around in.

Sarkar must have sensed my scepticism. 'Well, don't be obliged to answer now, man, I know you're bushed. Let's talk after the group-work submissions are over so we can book places in the course, get tickets and stuff.'

He didn't seem to be put off by my lack of enthusiasm. Sarkar and Vinod had been surprisingly patient when my need for space and privacy asserted itself periodically. Now was one of those times. My immediate problems were more material than spiritual—the lack of sleep, the consistent mediocrity and the most recent one: group project work.

Life would have been infinitely simpler if Sarkar, Vinod and I had been given a chance to stick together in all our group projects. But then, this place was not geared towards making life easier. In group-work intensive subjects like marketing, the professor created groups via a random selection process, saying, 'This will be a good experience because you almost never get a chance to pick your team at work—sometimes you need to deal with laziness, free riding, blatant insubordination and headstrong personalities.'

Seemed like my group was blessed with all those virtues, I thought during one particularly frustrating group assignment As luck would have it, Chetan and Nandini had ended up as part of the five-member group, and both threw dirty glances at me from time to time. Chetan had ended up with a job at a local bank for his internship and probably blamed me for missing the tube to London. Nandini had probably guessed that I had been high as a giraffe's balls during our date that night. The tension, therefore, was obvious as we worked together on the case study that night. Our task was to create a comprehensive marketing plan for a small regional cereal maker to help him expand his presence in the country, and our discussions went round and round in endless circles. Two o'clock in the morning and tempers were running high.

Finally, Lala ('Call me Archie'), a pompous English literature graduate from St Stephen's College in New Delhi and the fourth member of our illustrious group, opened the door to mayhem.

'Here, everyone, I don't think we've approached this in the correct manner. We need to think bigger, expand our horizons and have a more stretching vision. The cereal maker doesn't need a bunch of over-analytical business school grads to tell him to expand to just his neighbouring state.'

Chetan, who had painstakingly generated the complex data behind the limited-expansion model, took serious offence. He spewed venom: 'I'm sure he needs people who can't run a single calculation in their heads to read their poetry books and recommend impractical expansion strategies instead.'

I applauded him silently for diminishing the entire Bachelors of English Literature course to a poetry lesson.

But Lala was enraged, and his practised British accent quickly gave way to crude profanities.

'Just what have you achieved by running regression numbers all day anyway? Being a spreadsheet wizard and filling a bunch of Excel workbooks is GIGO: Garbage In, Garbage Out. Marketing requires innovation and you can't deliver that by jerking off all over numbers.'

Chetan, his face red, opened his mouth to reply when Nandini cut in. Despite our disaster date, I liked Nandini. She was ambitious and focused (which aren't necessarily bad traits unless you are a very particular kind of loser—a pampered American banker, a tortured Indian engineer or a misfit army officer, for example), yet she wasn't manically aggressive. She had good communication skills and a reasonably balanced, mature persona— all of which made her a very rare species at the IIM indeed. Usually she seemed pretty calm, but today was her meltdown day as well.

'Stop it, guys. Can we behave like adults? It's been three hours of vague, pointless discussions and we are getting nowhere. We haven't typed a word yet and the submission is due tomorrow, or damn, I guess it's due today, it's already 2 a.m. If we get started now, the earliest we can wrap up is by 4 a.m., and that is if we really start NOW. I am not prepared to talk any longer. I barely caught a wink of sleep yesterday and I need at least a couple of hours before the 8 a.m. accounting quiz.'

I agreed wholeheartedly. 'Personally, guys, I couldn't care a rat's ass what this cereal maker decides to do. It's his hell. Let's just take a call one way or the other, attach a couple of Excel files and be done with it.'

Chetan, clearly still carrying a grudge against me for denying him my valuable presence in his interview preparation, turned on me. 'Easy for you to say that. I would too, if I had Wall Street in one pocket and Shivam Chemicals in another. This case study is graded, and at least someone here needs to worry about grades.'

Boy, as the rednecks in Kentucky would say, you

couldn't swing a dead cat without hitting a touchy person today.

Dr Pal, the last member of our distinguished group, who'd been quiet so far, suddenly piped up: 'All I want to say is ki, I think there is a humanitarian aspect of business that the cereal maker should consider in his expansion plans. He should open his plants in Orissa, because generating employment in the poorest state of the country is the moral responsibility of a locally bred entrepreneur.' The doctor had raised yet another magnificently irrelevant point, and my stomach contracted with silent laughter.

Nandini missed the humour, though. She rose from the table, infuriated.

'I'm done, guys. I'll type the case on my own and in case you guys manage to get anything done, you can replace my case with yours. You can also choose not to have my name on it. I can live without grading for this assignment,' she said.

'I'll join you,' I said immediately. 'I'm at the bottom of the class, anyway. It's not like the gold medal is going to slip away from my hands if I don't get graded in this case.' I couldn't help but direct a small barb at Chetan's obsession with the gold medal.

Dr Pal rose as well. Lala and Chetan joined us after a moment's hesitation and we walked silently to the computer lab, rueing the day we had decided to pursue a business school degree. Under Nandini's military leadership, we suspended all attempts to think and diligently typed out our ten-page case analyses, dividing it among us in discrete sections so that there would be no more arguments. Chetan set the consumer context, Lala created the brand positioning, Nandini and I drafted the expansion strategy and Dr Pal prepared the media and advertising plans.

Our final case study had Chetan's detailed regression analyses that quantitatively rated the variables that most influence brand choices of cereal in India. The variable with the most impact on purchase turned out to be health benefits (almost a perfect correlation) and the least important, which had almost zero impact on purchase, were taste and packaging. However, the city-bred Lala's brand positioning reflected his personality and was all about hip, cool cereal with taste and packaging as the major differentiating factors. Our media plans, prepared by Dr Pal, focused on humanitarian, community-building efforts in states that our expansion plan didn't cover. For our core expansion strategy, Nandini and I had chosen to please everyone and recommended expanding to more than one state but not the whole country (this part of the case was not backed with any data, only vague qualitative rationale such as 'he should be ambitious but practical').

When we finally got done at 5 a.m., an hour later than planned, and collated the final case study, we realized it was a disaster. Okay, there goes the marketing course as well, I thought with a familiar sinking sensation, and the same thought seemed to be going through everyone's heads.

'We need to do the case again,' said Nandini. 'We can't submit it this way.'

I did a quick mental calculation. There were three hours left before the 8 a.m. accounting quiz. If I didn't go back and study for that. I would definitely get a D in the quiz. We were likely to get a D in the marketing case study as it stood currently and could probably manage a C if we tried to salvage it in the next couple of hours. What a conundrum: should I choose a C in accounting or marketing? I didn't want to be the rat that deserted the sinking ship, so I chose the C in marketing.

'But an hour means an hour, folks—no philosophical discussions, let's decide the main things to fix and attack it,' I said.

The 'main things to fix' turned out to be the whole case, of course. One hour turned into two, and then three as our aggressive, competitive selves got the better of us and we continued to nitpick and argue over the most inconsequential details.

'I think you are wrong. We should call it "healthy cereal" instead of "cereal for the healthy",' said Lala.

'Why?' said Chetan.

'It sounds better,' said Lala.

'No, cereal for the healthy sounds better. It calls the consumer healthy,' said Chetan.

'Why should they have our cereal if they are already healthy? Healthy cereal is better,' said Lala.

'But that implies they were unhealthy before they had our cereal. Let's stick with cereal for the healthy,' said Chetan.

'No, I think…' said Lala.

Very soon, I thought, unsuspecting shareholders would be paying them millions of dollars to have exactly such discussions.

When we rushed to take the prints twenty minutes before 8 a.m., the case analyses looked worse for our efforts over the past few hours. At least earlier we had had some innovative, though disconnected, ideas. Now we had diluted it to a blasé, still disjointed case study without a single original thought. But there was no other option than to submit it as it was.

Back in my room, I flipped through the pages of the accounting textbook half-heartedly. I gave up reading after a couple of minutes. There was no way I could manage to process anything in the ten minutes I had before the 8 a.m. quiz. On a whim, I decided to smoke a joint instead. What the heck, I thought, it will help me unwind, maybe even trigger off some hidden insight from class which might actually help in the quiz. I rolled a joint, noting proudly that my slow metamorphosis into becoming a manager had started. If I could convince myself that smoking up could actually help with a quiz, I could distort just about anything to prove my point. I felt pleased with myself. I was acquiring some real managerial traits; business school wasn't turning out to be a complete waste of time.

I glanced at the watch. 7:55 a.m. Five minutes left for the quiz. I should probably be making my way to the examination hall. But the joint seemed too good to let go. Heck, I thought, I could afford to be a couple of minutes late for the one-hour quiz, it wasn't like I had sixty minutes of sensible content to write. Just a couple of quick drags, and I would leave.

I watched the hands of the clock slowly hit 8 a.m. The quiz would have started, I thought vaguely, but I still had a ten-minute grace period before they shut the doors of the examination hall. I continued to observe the clock. I wondered briefly why the small hand of the clock denoted hours and the long hand minutes. Hours were longer than minutes, so shouldn't it be the other way around? I guess it was for the aesthetics; it probably looked more elegant this way. But fuck, it was a clock. At least a clock should be logical. Its primary duty was to restore some order to this disordered world. I was a bit annoyed by the clock so I got up to examine it. 8:20 a.m. It occurred to me that I had just given the accounting quiz a complete pass. I considered the irony of the situation. A former Yale valedictorian couldn't even be bothered to go for an examination in business school. Why? Because he was watching a fucking clock so intently that he didn't notice the time. That set me off, and I flopped on the bed laughing, out of control.

Somehow, I almost felt liberated. In a different life, I would have been in the examination hall, agonizing over the quiz, clocking time, unwilling to accept that I didn't know a damn thing being tested today. Now, I felt free enough to give up that pretence. I could spend the next forty minutes or so on more meaningful pursuits. Like smoking some more weed. I rolled another joint while contemplating how to spend my time most effectively.

What is it that would really please me, I wondered. There was no shortage of things to do, of course—assignments galore to finish, preparation for tomorrow's microeconomics quiz, getting organized for the end-terms, barely two weeks away. But I was stoned enough to admit to myself that I didn't really have to work all that hard to get a few more Cs and Ds. I was drowning anyway; a quiz here or there wasn't the straw that could save me. I thought of catching up on some sleep—I had slept less than three hours in the last forty-eight, but again, that seemed too petty a use of the forty delicious minutes of rare, complete solitude. I could go for a run—I had barely seen sunlight in the past twenty-four hours—but I wasn't quite ready to deal with the voices in my head.

Ultimately, I ended up calling Peter in Manhattan, trying my hardest to keep the desperation out of my voice. I envied his peace of mind. In the midst of superbusy million-dollar-earning-$5-Chinese-takeout-dinner-eating asshole bankers, here was a guy who could nonchalantly walk away from his office every evening at five, hit the bong, watch a Netflix flick and sleep a contented ten-hour sleep.

'Are you serious about your future?' one of the thousand vice-presidents in the bank had asked him once when he had brought a half-finished pitch book to some client meeting.

'Not really,' he had answered frankly.

That he would be fired was inevitable (and he was blissfully unconcerned about the same); the only question was when. Sometimes I thought he was just too lazy to fill out the paperwork required to resign.

It was late evening US time when I called and, as usual, he had time to spare. He didn't hound me about my many unanswered e-mails, or try to unearth the real cause for the momentary lapse of reason that led me to India.

'Finally, my man! Have you found out anything about yourself yet?' he said as soon as he picked up the phone.

The only thing I have found out about myself so far, I wanted to say, is that I like my joints best without the filter. No, wait. I've also found out that

I'm a natural, a real pro, at chasing a joint. Quite the self-discovery, wouldn't you say?

'Hardly,' I said. 'It hasn't been like I'd thought it would be. I guess Dad was right. What I'm seeking isn't in India.' I hesitated. 'It isn't anywhere, I guess. Probably inside me, corny though it sounds. Anyway, I'm not coming back anytime soon. I'm gonna give it a chance.'

'Come off it, dude,' he said. 'None of your bleakness please, especially now that you have become a role model for all the escapists of the world. With a single stroke, you've made finding oneself as hot as Paris Hilton's chihuahua. People have begun quitting left, right and centre taking inspiration from you. I just quit last month, am planning to backpack across Mongolia, Uzbekistan and Kyrgyzstan for a year.'

I smiled. So he had done it finally. We had been hitting the bong in a friend's room at Yale once when Peter had suddenly walked to the world map on the wall. He had pointed vaguely at Central Asia and said, 'This is where I'm gonna find it,' and kept repeating that for the rest of the night. He had omitted to explain what 'it' meant. It had been a recurrent theme since then. Whenever banking had become too mind-numbingly dull (which was always), Peter said that Mongolia was beckoning him and he would quit soon. He had done so now. I wished he would find in Mongolia what I hadn't found so far in India.

'Rocking,' I said. 'When are you leaving?'

'As soon as the Netflix queue runs out.' He laughed. 'You won't believe what happened.'

'What?'

'As soon as the markets imploded, they began offering golden handshakes. Guess who was first in line to ask for a package? I was about to quit for free, and then I was actually being offered money to quit!'

Talking to him was therapeutic. There was no inherent conflict in his life; no struggle between his good and his evil side, or his rational and his confused side, or his certainties and his insecurities. He was simple, contented, untormented by demons. Give him a bong, a Netflix movie, a ticket to Mongolia, and he didn't need a thing more. His contentedness was definitely infectious. By the time I came out of the phone booth, I didn't really care much about missing the accounting quiz any more.

However, my newfound bliss lasted only for a day, until we got our grades. I'd earned the double distinction of getting a D in both the accounting and marketing assignments. I also achieved yet another first in my academic career—being at the very bottom, bar none, in an examination.

'Even lower than Keshto, that stoned rocker dude who spends all his time strumming his guitar, singing Lennon's *Imagine* and chasing underage girls on the internet. He gets a D in everything, but even he managed a C. If I'd just come for the quiz, I would have probably managed a C too. Not that I would be awarded a gold medal for getting a C. But, still!' I complained to Vinod and Sarkar.

Vinod laughed. 'You take this stuff way too seriously. You're a prime candidate for the psychiatrist they've got here. Why don't you pay her a visit?'

I had visions of a sexy woman in an inviting office, beckoning me to her couch, and was immediately aroused. I felt ashamed—was I sex-starved or what? People needed counselling to stop themselves from committing suicide and all I could think about was getting a quickie.

'Have they got a shrink on campus?' Sarkar asked.

Sometimes I could swear that the bastard didn't live on the same planet as the rest of us. After Kunal's death, there had been notices all over campus about the appointment of the new guidance counsellor to help students deal with stress.

'We don't need a psychiatrist,' Sarkar continued, 'we all know what the problems are, but they're so endemic that nobody can fix them.'

'And what are the problems, Doctor Sarkar?' Vinod asked mockingly.

Sarkar launched into his usual treatise about the sorry state of the system. 'Well, the fundamental issue is that most of us are misfits here. None of us actively made a choice to study in business school. Take my roommate there, for example. He wanted to study literature or journalism after school, become a writer one day. Do you know what his father said? "Son, all people in India want to read about is whether Dharmendra lives with Hema Malini or his first wife, and whether Amitabh had an affair with Rekha. Do you really want to study Milton and Shakespeare for three years to write about that?" My friend was so impressed with his father's knowledge of Bollywood, he listened to him and ended up at IIT instead. And now he writes software code for a company that makes lubricating oil, after dreaming all his life of writing fiction. How do we expect him to be happy here? And what can a psychiatrist do about it?'

I almost laughed. The saga of his friend sounded more comic than tragic.

'Sarkar, you bastard,' Vinod said, 'you are the biggest whiner in the world. I haven't heard a single positive thing from you in the last three months. Come on, boy, see the light. This isn't some job that you can quit to find another one. It's life; you have to live it. You don't have an option, so can't you quit complaining?'

I agreed with Vinod. What right did Sarkar have to complain anyway? He was acing the course while I was trying to claw my way up from the bottom.

'Seriously, man, I think I just need a break,' Sarkar said.

There he goes again, I thought, another break. He always needed a break. What from—smoking up, popping pills, listening to rock and acing the course? I wish I had that kind of stress in my life.

'Let's just get out of campus for a while,' he suggested.

'I second that,' Vinod said.

They turned to me. End-term examinations began in less than two weeks.

'Okay, I guess,' I said, suddenly feeling the urge to get out of campus as well. Did it matter whether I was ranked 90th in a class of two hundred, or 120th? No one was dispensing honorary degrees to the first hundred of the class. If you weren't in the top ten, your rank was just a number.

I should have figured a crazy, madcap idea was in the works when Sarkar convinced us to take an auto-rickshaw instead of his beloved bike. But I shouldn't be too hard on myself. Because what we did next was so beyond my sphere of comprehension that I never could have hazarded a guess anyway.

Sarkar told the auto-rickshaw driver to head for the airport.

'Now what? Getting stoned and watching planes land? Very unoriginal,' Vinod said.

'Nope, bigger game.' Sarkar waved his newly acquired Citibank credit card which a company had doled out to all business school students to start getting them hooked to credit for life. 'We take the first flight that leaves from Bangalore, wherever it goes. What do you think of that?'

Vinod seemed to like the plan. 'Very cool, boss. We will be back tomorrow, right? Today is gone anyway. Might as well go to a new city instead of going to a pub again. Let's take a bet on where we will end up. A bet on the credit card, of course, I don't have any money of my own,' Vinod said.

Some folks at the IIM used the credit card to buy books to supplement their coursework, others used it to buy formal suits for interviews, we used it to get stoned in a new city. I felt proud. We were the dream customers of credit card companies— spendthrifts, irresponsible and reckless.

The complete randomness of the journey titillated me, and I complained just once that night when our destination turned out to be the desert city of Jodhpur in Rajasthan. I learnt that the flight would follow a circuitous connection via Delhi, which would further eat into the few hours we would have to spend there.

'This isn't the way to see Rajasthan,' I whined. 'Americans dream all their lives of coming to India to see Rajasthan's palaces. It is simply moronic to see it like this in one evening.'

'Come on, *firang*, you can always see the pictures of palaces in the guidebooks. I promise this way we will see the real Rajasthan,' Sarkar said.

'Balls. Jodhpur isn't the real Rajasthan,' Vinod said. 'It is okay for those who can't make the journey into the Thar desert, I guess. The real Rajasthan is in Jaisalmer. I know it well, I did a military exercise there.'

Our quest for the 'real Rajasthan' took on a new dimension of absurdity as we shook awake a dead-drunk cabdriver to take us to Jaisalmer after our flight finally touched down in Jodhpur at 8 p.m.

I couldn't help myself. 'This is just crazy, guys,' I said. 'Are we going to drive for five hours just to have a cup of tea in Jaisalmer? In the unlikely case that we do make it there alive, we will have to drive back immediately to board the early-morning flight back to Bangalore, right? Just what is the point?'

'Don't exaggerate,' Vinod said. 'We will have more time than that in Jaisalmer. We can probably squeeze in time for a bite.'

'Great,' I said, 'if we can have some toast and omelette in Jaisalmer, the ten-hour round trip definitely seems worth it.'

'Chill, maachi check,' Sarkar said, 'just sit in the car, smoke a joint and watch the stars. It will be well worth it just for that.'

He did have a point. The stars seemed exceptionally bright in the pristine Rajasthan sky, and I settled down in the backseat of the Toyota and rolled down the window. The soft, cool desert breeze, the steady hum of the car's engine, wisps of Sarkar and Vinod's conversations and the absolute purposelessness of the journey lulled me into a comfortable, dreamy stupor. I sat comatose, staring at the hypnotic twinkling of the stars from my window, and nodded off from time to time. We reached Jaisalmer earlier than expected and gave the city a pass to drive on for an hour, further into the desert.

It was past midnight, but Vinod convinced us to take a camel ride into the desert. We woke up a couple of stoned camel owners. Sarkar brought out a couple of joints for the journey and I smoked one before mounting my camel. The camel let out a sudden snort, and I looked at it closely. I had never seen a camel before, let alone been on top of one. It was such a majestic, yet oddly shaped animal. I tried to analyse what was so irregular about it. It was... well, asymmetrical, like a giraffe. Any way you tried, you couldn't slice it in equal, even halves. Slicing camels reminded me of Peter, who had said that they ate camels in Mongolia. Peter would have enjoyed this ride, I thought, and somehow this made me happy. Soon, I began to enjoy the crazy, rhythmic sway of the camel's long strides through the vast, unending expanse of sand lit by the soft glow of moonlight. 'Beautiful' is perhaps too hackneyed a word to express the miles and miles of absolute, complete desolation that stretched before us. It was... was psychedelic, like a trip in the head versus an actual, physical journey.

Our midnight excursion took another surreal turn when our guides made for a camp set up by a tribe of gypsies. The tourists had long gone for the

day and the banjaaras were sitting peacefully around
a fire, swigging hooch and breaking into impromptu
dances. Everyone looked pleasantly stoned and
(probably recognizing fellow spirits) welcomed us
in. Splendidly clad women in their colourful, shiny
clothes, welcoming white canvas tents, a warm fire,
the hypnotic dancing—it was, I thought, almost like
a scene from an ancient Egyptian porn movie, like
a Pharaoh's harem, if there ever was such a thing.
We joined them around the fire. This was one way
to live, I thought as I looked around, and a good
one at that. Settle down in a place for a while. And
when the monotony becomes unbearable, pack
your belongings and move again. Alive and free, no
attachments, wandering from nowhere to nowhere,
living only in the present moment, the future too
unpredictable to plan for or be concerned about.

Vinod interrupted my thoughts. 'Read his hand.
He has the most questions,' Vinod was saying to an
old gypsy woman sitting next to me.

Her eyes twinkled and her crusty, wrinkled face
came alive. She looked hard and beautiful. 'They
have the gift of reading the future,' he explained
to me. I must have looked sceptical. 'Suspend your
American disbelief and listen to her, you bastard.
She knows more about you than you know about
yourself.'

She asked me in her musical accent if I was
right-handed, and then held my left hand. ('The

left is what the gods give you, the right is what you do with it,' she said.) Her hands felt surprisingly smooth, despite appearing wrinkled and callused. She studied my left palm for a while, looked puzzled and then asked for my right palm. She scrutinized it intensely. Then she went back to the left again.

'You have a funny hand,' she said.

My scepticism had given way to suspense now. She was silent and confident, and obviously knew what she was doing. Hello, am I gonna die soon? Please let me know so I can get the fuck away from B-school and live my last days in peace.

'The left hand which represents your destiny promises success and happiness. Your right hand, your actions, just the opposite. It looks as if you are fighting your destiny when you shouldn't be doing so. Just let it go, that's the best I can say to you. Just let it go.'

❃

We were back on campus the next day. I wish I could say that the gypsy's prophecy in Rajasthan led to a dramatic change in my life after we returned. But this isn't a fairy tale and no such thing happened. End-terms were approaching, the days and nights merged into one long nightmare of frenzied activity and I sleepwalked through the remainder of the term. All the talk about 'letting go' was fine as long as I could graduate from school, and the fear that I would not lurked in my mind. The Jaisalmer experience had given me a taste of India though, and each day, I awaited the beginning of my ten-day hiatus in Dharamsala after the examination. I wanted so badly to be free, to live a normal, unregimented life, and ten days in a quaint Himalayan town promised all that and more.

8

A Normal, Unregimented Life?

Finally the first term, the longest three months of my life, was over. I was in a state of happy delirium in the last thirty minutes of the final exam—organizational behaviour—and decided to do a Sarkar on the last question, 'Detriments of technology on communication'. I blasted the topic, stating that technology—e-mail, BlackBerry devices, voicemails etc.—was in fact the best invention in a manager's life and ridiculed the shallowness of those who thought otherwise. I was damned if I cared about my grades in OB after I had already bungled the Big Three—accounting, statistics and economics.

The campus came back to life after the last exam as everyone partied hard that night before taking off the next morning for the safe cocoon of their homes. I felt a momentary pang as I thought of Mom and Dad back home in the US. What I badly needed right now was the comfort of my old room, to sleep for an eternity tucked under my blanket, to wake up to a mug of hot coffee from Mom and walk with Dad in the snow. No matter what had gone wrong in my spoiled little life—having my undergraduate application rejected by Harvard, losing Sarah, my first serious love, a spare episode of racism, politics at work—things were always fine at home. I no longer had that protective cushion, and I certainly didn't want to go looking for comfort with my various aunts and uncles who lived in India. I had made my choices and needed to live with them, though I did envy Vinod as he left, overjoyed, for his home in Ambala.

'We are going to play big games in the mountains. You should come with us,' Sarkar had mockingly invited him knowing he would never come for something as intangible as a meditation course.

Vinod just shook his head at our foolishness. 'What's the big game in turning down ten days of my mother's food and living in a hostel again? Of course, if you learn to fly on a carpet at the end of ten days, come and pick me up. I'm so broke I could do with a free ride.'

Instead of a flying carpet though, Sarkar and I found ourselves on an arduously long thirty-hour train journey from Bangalore to Pathankot. If I had any apprehensions about surviving the squalor of a crowded second-class compartment in an Indian train with peanut shells, banana skins, orange pips, tea and water strewn all over the floor, they were soon dismissed. Almost immediately after we'd had our tickets checked and settled down next to the airless ceiling on the upper berth, I drifted into a long, death-like sleep. I woke with a start as I felt myself being sucked into an airless vortex, pulled deeper and deeper towards a gigantic mouth waiting to devour me. ('What a bastard of a dream. Must have been IIM tormenting me in my sleep,' I told Sarkar later.) I glanced at Sarkar who was still sleeping in the neighbouring seat, and soon fell back into an exhausted sleep, too drained to move.

We were finally shaken awake by an attendant, who had been summoned by fellow passengers who feared we were drugged, or worse, dead. A quick glance at my watch showed that we had been asleep for nearly twelve hours straight. The Punjabi family on the berths below smiled through their pooris and aloo-bhaji on seeing us up. It was obvious they were bursting with curiosity, but I wasn't in the mood to bare my soul to them. In the midst of their collective 'wow' as Sarkar informed them that we were from IIM, I gestured to him for a cigarette.

Sarkar didn't look pleased as he made for the door, next to the stinking toilets. 'She was cute, yaar. I could have scored. I badly need some action,' he said, referring to the eldest daughter of the family who was reasonably good-looking in a plump, Punjabi way. He held out his pack of cigarettes, himself pulling out a joint.

'Hey, is it legal to smoke even a cigarette on the train?' I asked him looking at the 'No Smoking' signs on the walls.

'Yes, of course,' Sarkar replied, the consummate expert on the Indian legal system. By now, I should have known better than to be surprised by this. 'Let me show you one of the greatest joys of life,' he said as he opened the door of the moving train, letting in a sudden blast of cool air which almost blew me away. But he wasn't planning to jump. We proceeded to sit on the doorstep with the wind blowing against our faces as the train sped past the wild, beautiful landscape.

The combination of the overwhelming relief that we had survived our first term, the many uninterrupted hours of sleep and the abundant supply of marijuana turned out to be ideal fuel for some stimulating conversation. It was evening, and our train was supposed to arrive only late in the morning the following day.

'Dude,' I asked Sarkar, 'Tell me more about Dharamsala. What are you hoping to get there? I mean, it seems woefully out of character for you.'

'Hmm… let's see. First I need another joint,' he replied.

Soon we were sitting there in total bliss, watching the harsh landscape go by, beautiful in its lack of structure or organization. Unlike the US, there were no roadside landmarks like McDonald's or Walmarts or IHOPs to give you the uneasy feeling that you can run but never really escape—everywhere you go is a crushing mass of sameness. In India, I thought, every bit is different from the rest because something unique has happened there—maybe a fire burnt down a field, or a tree crashed and blocked a road or someone decided to open a dhaba or a paan shop in the middle of nowhere, or a random group of farmers settled down to play cards in the field at dusk. Through a haze, I saw the fields merge into one giant gorgeous landmass that seemed to be rushing away from the train, and I wondered vaguely about the theory of relativity. I thought of how good I had been at science in high school and wondered whether it had been a mistake to get into finance and business. Maybe I should have stuck to science—become an astronaut and escaped into space. Maybe I would have had a female astronaut as my buddy, and we could have had weightless sex in space, the ultimate kink experience.

Such happy thoughts chased each other in my head. It was an undeniably good life, I thought eventually, and there is some joy in not knowing all the answers. I wouldn't want to exchange the confusions in my head with the anticlimactic certainty of knowing everything. That would kill the joy of this quest, I thought, with a sudden burst of optimism.

'What are you smiling about?' Sarkar said.

'Nothing, just taking stock. Anyway, to go back to what you were saying, what are you hoping to get there?' I asked.

Sarkar paused as he usually did before launching into a long, profound monologue, and took another drag.

'Look, for a long time, I thought I had all the answers to everything, that it could all be worked out scientifically, life and God and all. But then recently, I heard this Goenka chap say somewhere, "The quest for the infinite can't be fulfilled by the finite." That struck a chord. I realized I was deluding myself by intellectualizing everything, trying to create complex theories about the nature of truth, none of which were even remotely satisfying. Goenka seemed to know something I didn't know. So I decided to suspend judgement and see what the course has to offer. Simple.'

'Hardly simple! Who's got the time to make up theories about existence when just living takes so much effort? Not me, for sure. I'm a shallow American, after all.' I grinned. 'Anyway, tell me more. What theory did you come up with about God? I always thought of you as an atheist.'

'Well, I do believe in God, but not as an entity to worship or fear. I believe in His existence as a mathematical concept—an originating force, after which the rules of mathematics and science take over. Good balances evil, creation balances destruction, happiness balances suffering—and after that the universe rolls on without God's assistance or interference. For every Hitler, there will be a Mother Teresa, for every person dying of poverty in India, there will be a Warren Buffet making billions in the US, for every selfish Chetan, there is a bighearted Vinod Singh, and so on. That explained a lot of things for me. For example, why is the leper on the Calcutta street dying in squalor? It is because Warren Buffet is in his Omaha mansion, being sucked off by his secretary. And why is there suffering for the leper and prosperity for Warren Buffet? Well, mathematics again. If we think of the soul as having many different lives, then on average the soul will be right in the centre. There will be lifetimes in which the soul comes as a leper, and lifetimes in which it comes as a rich bastard, but the net of all the deviations will be in the centre. Not making much sense, am I?' Sarkar said.

'No, no. Go on. This is interesting,' I said, meaning it.

'Well, that's really the end of it. So... well, I tried to believe in my theory, but then I realized that all this big talk is just crap. For all my theories, I'm not at peace, and I'm sure there is something I'm missing. And it can't be found sitting lotus-style in my room reading heavy books,' Sarkar said.

Suddenly, incomprehensibly, I thought of the *Matrix*. In a way, Sarkar was like the Neo of *Matrix* or the Frodo Baggins of *The Lord of the Rings*, an unlikely hero on an unknown but important quest. Of course, Sarkar didn't behave like a hero—all he ever did was smoke, get drunk and bitch about the system. However, his relentless search for meaning would eventually lead him to the right door, I thought. And once there, maybe he would do something profound and dramatic, perhaps with consequences for the world at large. I didn't reveal my thoughts to Sarkar though, as we made our way back to our seats for the night. It was probably necessary for him to run after illusions of happiness for now—IIT, IIM, a banking internship in London—before he eventually found what mattered. Or perhaps I was being dramatic as usual. He could just be a stoned pop philosopher after all.

'My reasons for coming here are nowhere as deep, you know,' I said. 'But I must mention—and I don't even know if this has any relevance—the character I related to the most in the *Matrix* was the traitor who ratted on Neo and his friends. Don't remember his name, but I recall what he said. Something like, "I know this piece of chicken isn't real, but I enjoy its taste so much that I don't care." I think I'm like that. I know there is a deeper secret, and what is apparent is not really real but I don't care enough to find out. In a perverse kind of way, I enjoy my self-doubts and confusion so much that I don't want to let go of them. Anyway, to hell with the pop philosophy. What are the chances of getting some action in Dharamsala?'

❈

We changed at Delhi for an overnight train to Pathankot and then took a bus to Dharamsala. Ignoring the solicitations of the hundred-odd rickshaw-drivers who descended upon us at the bus stand in Dharamsala, we elected to walk to our destination.

'It's the only way to see the real India,' said Sarkar. 'Either that, or stoned on a bike.'

Flashes from the past again: walking and biking with Peter and Radha across Cambodia, Vietnam and Thailand after graduation.

'It all goes downhill from here,' Peter had said at the end of the trip, 'adulthood and responsibility, mortgages, kids, financial planning, the works. From now on, happiness will mean remembering the ghosts of our time in Yale.'

Peter had been right. Things had gone downhill from there even though I had effectively managed to shirk all responsibility. I always ran at the first sign of it—exited relationships when they demanded commitment, ended friendships when they called for an investment of time and abandoned my career when it was about to go places.

For now though, I thought ironically, I'm going uphill. As we started our climb to the town, I was surprised to see more Westerners than Indians almost everywhere in the small picturesque Himalayan town.

'It's a dope haven,' Sarkar explained. 'It grows its own stuff so marijuana is easily accessible and cheap.

Attracts a lot of foreigners.' At least Sarkar was getting something out of business school, I thought, he seemed to have mastered the entire supply chain, distribution and marketing framework of marijuana in India.

I also saw many signs for meditation classes.

'The entrepreneurial Indian.' Sarkar was quick with an explanation again. 'Where there is a buck to be made, they'll make it. There is a ton of money to be made in the spiritual rap. Very low investment— get a bunch of idiots together in an auditorium, play a pirated tape with eerie music, mutter "Om" a couple of times, scream in orgasmic ecstasy, provide stripped-down living quarters in the name of austerity and promise a piece of soul to the soulless foreigners if they pay enough. Very high returns— you get paid in dollars for the scam.'

The whole town radiated a tense, frenzied energy as locals accosted foreigners with cheap bargains on food, accommodation, dope, sex and salvation. No one paid much attention to us. We looked like what we were—penniless students, without even the means to buy a first-class train ticket. Only the ubiquitous pimps, who immediately figured the equation—Two Indian Males = Desperate for Sex—tried to entice us. Words I had heard before were repeated: 'Foreigner. Rs 1,000, all night.'

We ignored them and made our way out of the busy town. The Vipaasana meditation centre was a couple of miles away and even higher up. It felt terrific to be in the mountains again and get some exercise. I had very specific objectives for the next ten days—run in the mountains, catch up on my reading, get stoned, sleep a lot, talk to the locals and spare whatever little time was left to this meditation gig.

The Vipaasana centre, however, had other plans. As soon as we signed in, the instructors laid down the ground rules. For ten days we had to maintain complete silence, no verbal or nonverbal communication, no reading or writing, no running, jogging or other exercise, no smoking, drinking and of course no pot, no dinner, just two meals a day. The schedule stated that we had to wake up every day at 4 a.m., meditate for two hours, break for breakfast, meditate again for three hours, break for lunch, meditate for five more hours, attend a discourse by Goenka and go to bed by 10 p.m. So there would be six hours of sleep every day and barring the small breakfast and lunch breaks, we would pretty much meditate for the remaining eighteen.

I pulled Sarkar aside. 'What have you got us into? I'd planned on running and getting stoned in the mountains, but this is as bad as school. I'm getting out of here!'

Sarkar confessed, 'I wasn't completely transparent, I know. I did guess you couldn't run here, but I hadn't bargained for the vow of silence. Anyway, we've come all this way, let's just flow with it for a while and we can leave in the middle if we have to.'

I relented. Goenka was about to address the hundred people or so who had signed up for the course. Sarkar had been right about him. A short bald man, he had a supremely peaceful, contented look on his face. He definitely didn't look like the kind who would have to be pulled away from an orgy by his attendant so that he could quickly button up and preach the virtues of chastity to his unsuspecting class. Here was a man who looked like he had figured it out, I thought, and I liked him immediately. Still, an effective teacher doesn't make an effective course. Remember financial accounting, boy?

The calm in Goenka's voice was enviable.

'You're all here for different reasons,' he began, 'but your underlying motivation is the same.'

My underlying motivation, I thought as I scanned the lecture hall hungrily, is to father the children of that voluptuous dusky woman sitting across from me. Can your meditation course arrange for that to happen, please?

'You are here,' Goenka continued, 'because you're fairly restless, somewhat dissatisfied... searching but not knowing what to search for. Happy, perhaps, but at a loss to understand what happiness really means. Am I right?'

I stopped staring at the woman. He had my attention.

'I don't think this ten-day course will change that, but it will definitely give you a glimpse of the solution. I'm on the journey myself, quite far from the destination, but I'm certain that this path is the right one,' he continued.

I believed him. He exuded a warmth that convinced me there wasn't a fake bone in his body.

Goenka then went on to explain what Vipaasana meditation meant, and his explanation appealed to my scientific side. Through a series of breathing techniques, the meditation establishes that even the smallest cell in the body is constantly changing, forcing the mind to recognize that the physical 'me' it knew a nanosecond ago was different from the physical 'me' it knows now. Realizing this impermanence of the physical form ensures that the mind doesn't get attached to all the material comforts that the body seeks—wealth, power, fame, money, sex, etc.—the hunger for which is the root cause of all dissatisfaction. The act of the mind transcending all material cravings and becoming one with the universal soul, never to be born again in the human form, is nirvana, enlightenment or liberation. Easier said than done, though. Goenka didn't promise enlightenment like a dandruff shampoo's '100% flake-free hair in ten days' guarantee. He was realistic and, in fact, somewhat pessimistic about the end state (consider these remarks from him—'Few are called, fewer are chosen', 'It may take several lifetimes to accomplish the goal', etc).

By the time we went back to the dormitory, I had made up my mind to stay. Listening to Goenka had made me hopeful, something I hadn't felt in a long time. There were answers out there if you really made a choice to seek them, I thought. Some people like Goenka had the courage to do so, and the results were obvious. Sarkar seemed to feel the same. 'This Goenka chap is like a small boy running barefoot on the beach with waves softly washing over his feet—no baggage, no struggles, completely, absolutely free,' he said.

I embarked on an unexpected spiritual quest from there even as I struggled to transition from an overactive, restless lifestyle to one of quiet, constant meditation. Despite sleep here being even more difficult than it was in business school (hours of constant meditation dramatically energized me), my thoughts in bed were active, happy and positive. I forgave even the hippie Westerner sleeping next to me in the dormitory room who always emanated a sour, dirty smell, like curd. He must be 'Kurdish', I thought, and collapsed into helpless, silent giggles at my private joke. Happiness means calling someone who smells like sour curd a Kurd instead of cursing the bastard, I thought, and laughed some more.

As the days went by, I began to feel calmer and happier than I had felt any time before. On the third day I had, or rather I imagined I had, a transcendental experience just as I was drifting off to sleep. A sudden energy seemed to radiate through my whole body, filling my mind with a sense of complete, absolute peace. I floated deliriously, light-headed, all my senses suddenly, intensely acute. It didn't happen again, but that day was the turning point, and meditating afterwards filled me with a rare sense of contentment and bliss.

As the tenth day dawned, I felt a massive pang of regret at having to go back to the frenzied pace of soulless activity at the IIM. I was happy here, meditating, listening to discourses, not speaking to a soul, eating the strictly vegetarian food and feeling fitter, healthier and happier by the moment. I debated for a second whether I should stay on. Should I go back to being a mouse in a B-school rat race, or should I try to achieve enlightenment —get mukti from the cycle of birth and death that binds us humans? There couldn't have been a clearer choice.

And of course, once again, I didn't make the clear choice. At the end of the tenth day, I found myself outside the centre, waiting patiently for Sarkar. We exchanged notes about our stay, but soon fell silent, our experiences too intensely personal to discuss. Instead, we talked of comfortable trivialities.

'Did you notice there were only four or five Indians and at least a hundred foreigners in our class?' Sarkar said. 'Ironically, more foreigners are interested in historical, cultural and spiritual India than Indians are. As Westerners flock to India for spiritual awakening, we go there for all the gross material things they set out to escape—a house in the suburbs, two cars in the garage and easy access to *Playboy*, *Penthouse* and strip clubs. It's pretty fucked, if you think about it.'

I didn't feel like getting into any deep stuff then. Ten days of intense self-reflection were enough to last me for some time. 'Dude, what's our plan of action? We don't have reservations for the trip back, remember?'

'No, man, but we can easily pay off the ticket collector and get a berth to sleep. Let's play it by ear,' Sarkar replied. 'Want to catch a beer first?'

I hesitated. Goenka had suggested quitting drinking, drugs and smoking, all vices that distract the soul from its higher pursuits. More than that though, in the last ten days I had experienced the joy of living a pure life, a high in not seeking a high. Abstinence felt right, not just something I ought to do.

'Come on,' said Sarkar, as if reading my thoughts. 'Abstinence will require effort, and I am sure IIM won't give us a chance to make that effort. Maybe after we graduate, yes?'

Perhaps it was his sound logic or perhaps it was the uncomfortable feeling of behaving like a recovering Bible belt 'I found Jesus' alcoholic, but I gave in and let gross, material desires vanquish whatever little spiritual progress I had made in Dharamsala.

We stopped at a small dhaba and ordered a spread of spicy chhole-bhature and paneer parathas (ignoring Goenka's rule about sticking to simple, saatwik food) and some beer (another tenet broken). We smoked a quiet cigarette (one more!), enjoying the immediate hit, and were making plans to source dope (yet another!) before our train ride back to Bangalore when—

'Weren't you guys at the Vipaasana course?' asked a sexy voice in a thick European accent. We turned to see a twenty-something buxom brunette who had been with us in the course. Sex was the final craving that Goenka had asked us to abstain from, now I was eager to break this last tenet immediately.

'Yes, we were, but don't take this meal as an indication of how much impact the course had on us.' I smiled. 'Why don't you join us?' Vipaasana notwithstanding, I was now stirred by the thought of getting some action after months of celibacy. What a cheap pervert I've become, I thought. Why does Westerner = sex come to my mind here in India, despite having spent an entire lifetime in the US? It's all India's fault, I concluded, women are just too prudish and inhibited here. So the country was to blame, not me. I was a manager after all, and managers are never at fault. If you look hard enough, there is always someone to blame.

Roxanne was from Denmark and had been living in India for several months. She was planning to backpack her way from Dharamsala to Tibet and then Nepal. She was surprised to know that we were business school students.

'But that is so different from everything that Vipaasana teaches. Don't business schools teach you to worship money and all the other things that come with it—power, ambition and fame?'

'Yes, they do. All that and more,' Sarkar replied. 'We're the tortured misfits who came here to escape that. What do you do?'

'I'm a philosophy grad from the University of Copenhagen,' she replied. 'I'm taking a year off to travel the world. I teach English in a local school here but I'm leaving soon for Tibet. Actually, I'm leaving tomorrow.'

We chatted for a long time—about Vipaasana, India, Western and Eastern philosophy, hiking, backpacking, B-school, the emptiness of life—everything. Conversation, alcohol and cigarettes flowed freely. I was having visions of hiking with her in the icy slopes of the Himalayas in Tibet and making love in a warm, cosy tent when she broke my reverie.

'It's been great talking to you guys. You know you won't believe this, but I haven't ever actually sat and conversed with locals about anything meaningful. Before coming here, I was warned that most locals think of Westerners as ATM machines or sex objects, and we were told to avoid them as much as possible. But I'm so lucky to have found you guys on my very last day here. I really did want to meet locals—there is no fun in hanging out with your own people, especially when you are in a country as diverse as India.'

I felt ashamed. I was guilty of neglecting to mention that I was actually American. Yet, I didn't want Sarkar to communicate this to her.

'Well, we're not exactly locals…' Sarkar began, but I signalled to him to shut up. 'Whatever,' I rationalized to myself, 'my accent screams I am American, and if she really can't tell, it's all the best for her.' Whatever floats her boat, I thought.

She went on, 'My friends here are meeting tonight for a sort of a farewell party. Why don't you join us? We would love to get to know you guys.'

So we ended up staying an extra day in Dharamsala instead of rejoining school on time. At least our priorities were clear. We made our way to Roxy's one-bedroom apartment on top of a hill. Our going-away present for her was a pound of hash we'd secured from a local dealer, which was greeted with great excitement by her friends. They were mostly European, American and Israeli hippie bums ('We are children of Tierre Madre, Mother

Earth,' they told us)—excellent company for an evening. We strummed on the guitar, traded stories of our spiritual experiences and our interpretations of the universal questions of 'Who am I? Why did I come here? What is this world? Who is the creator?' while passing around the hash. Sarkar, who was in his element, delighted the hippies with a rare glimpse into his twisted world.

'Shambhu, Shambhu. This is the ultimate truth,' said a dreadlocked American as he absorbed Sarkar's 'God is a mathematical equation' bullshit.

'Prabhu. You are… God. I have nothing more to live for,' said an Israeli stoner, crashing on Sarkar's feet.

In the meantime, I had been busy reading everyone's body language to figure out if anyone showed a level of intimacy that could qualify him as being Roxanne's boyfriend. To my utter delight, there seemed to be none. As the night progressed into early morning, I decided to regress back to being the pervert I was. I approached Roxanne.

'Hey, do you want to go for a short walk?'

'Sure. And listen, thanks so much for agreeing to come—you guys made the party special. My friends just loved hearing your experiences.'

We chatted for a while about her travels, her life back in Denmark. I was keenly aware of the increasing sexual tension between us as we kept walking in the bracing mountain air. We had walked a couple of miles downhill to the main Dharamsala city when she stopped.

'I can't walk any further. Should we just take a hotel tonight and stay here?' she asked.

I looked to see if she was flirting, but her expression didn't give away anything.

'Sure, but I don't think I have enough cash for two rooms.'

She seemed fine with that as we stopped at a seedy hotel and checked in with the desk clerk, who gave me a knowing smirk. On the way to the room Roxanne kissed me lightly and I was immediately aroused. Abandoning all attempts to hide my true intentions, I kissed her passionately, gently fondling her big, soft breasts through the thin fabric of her dress as I shut the door of the room. I admitted to her that I had wanted her the moment I had set eyes on her at the dhaba.

'Even I have wanted to make love to an Indian ever since I came here, but have been scared off by everyone… except now,' she replied, smiling.

I felt another momentary pang at the fact that I wasn't really Indian but not enough to pull away from the moment.

We slowly undressed each other and I paused to admire her narrow waist, wide hips and tight, well-toned calves. She pulled me close to her and we made intense, silent, unhurried love. Perhaps it was the several months of celibacy or perhaps it was me distorting Goenka's 'Live in the moment' philosophy, but I had arguably the best sex of my life in that room with its dirty pink bedsheets and bare hardwood floor. Satiated and spent, we lay naked and smoked a cigarette as we joked about breaking every holy tenet that we had learnt in our ten days of Vipaasana meditation. Since we met, we had shared alcohol, hash, cigarettes and now sex, with the knowledge that there never would be a next time. I hoped she wouldn't conduct the charade of exchanging e-mail addresses and promising to keep in touch—our brief interlude was perfect just the way it was. She didn't.

'Should we start making a move back?' she said. 'I hope the party in my house is still under control.' I hadn't realized it was dawn already.

We walked back, enjoying the splendid mountain sunrise, and came home to Sarkar lecturing the hippies on the importance of leaving the cultural depravation of the West for (the cultural depravation of) the East. Trance music, heavy fumes and couples cosied up in corners formed the background to this scene, which seemed zillions of miles away from the life to which we were about to return. I wanted to follow Roxanne to Tibet and Nepal and make love to her every night in the Himalayas. Sarkar wanted to stay on in Dharamsala and continue with the Vipaasana meditation course for a lifetime. Neither of us had the balls to make those choices, so we made our way back to Bangalore, profoundly unhappy at having to return.

The next semester had better be worth all the spiritual and sexual sacrifices we were making for it, I thought during the miserable ticketless journey from Pathankot to Bangalore. And physical too, I reminded myself, as I sat on the floor outside the dirty bathroom in the inhumanly crowded general compartment of the train. Sarkar, the bastard, had lost his touch and couldn't persuade the ticket collector to give us a seat. It was because I had spent all our remaining money on the hash and the hotel room, he reminded me.

The next semester had better be worth it, I thought again.

9

The Next Semester Had Better Be Worth It

The next two semesters were marginally better than the first. This had less to do with the pace of the coursework—which remained consistently brutal—and more to do with us slowly getting comfortable in our own skins. Like Bud Fox in *Wall Street* ('As much as I wanted to be Gordon Gekko, I will always be Bud Fox') I slowly started accepting my strengths, of which there weren't many, and 'improvement areas' —managers never use terms like weakness and failures, of course, no matter how screwed you are—which proved abundant.

Thanks to our exertions in Dharamsala, we missed the announcement of the grade point averages from the first term. But Sarkar's 3.8 GPA, just marginally behind the top ranker, had already made news. I shook my head in awe when I recalled the nights he had spent stoned while the rest of us had continued to slog in quiet desperation. Life just isn't meant to be fair, I thought for the millionth time since

I'd met him. I had scored a 2.9, ranking ninetieth in the class of 200, slightly better than halfway, which pleasantly surprised me. (How the mighty have fallen! From Yale valedictorian to finding it 'pleasantly surprising' to be in the top 50 per cent of the class, I thought.)

Vinod had managed a 3.20, ranked sixtieth—a very formidable position (by our standards). Chetan was third, after Sarkar. He was no doubt displeased by his performance, especially because his rock-playing pothead of a neighbour had pipped him to the post with no apparent effort whatsoever.

Don't worry, I wanted to tell him, it is so much easier to slip into mediocrity. There is no longer the pressure to monitor every test score and worry about someone usurping your lonely position at the top. Ask me, the resident expert on slipping down that slope. In fact, I actually felt liberated now from the monotony of chasing grades, keeping score and pining for medals. I looked forward to the pure joy of learning once again, whatever that meant.

Vinod seemed to have applied this principle with some success as well. According to him, he 'aced' the end-term examinations (again, our definition) after middling through most of the term because, 'Big game, boss. I think I've hit upon a formula for success. I try to think of myself as the protagonist of every case study. In statistics, for instance, I thought of myself as Chubby Charlie, the hero of

Prof. Dasgupta's case studies, and somehow this helped me construct that decision-tree to divide pizza slices. It helped in managerial accounting the most actually. I really started to think of Sears Co. as my own company and treated every entry in the balance sheet as if it would impact my personal profit and loss statement. It just provides a different dimension to the course and makes it come alive instead of being just numbers on a page. Believe me, boss, you should try it too. We don't have much to lose anyway.'

He had a point. Given a chance, B-school curriculum can be remarkably interesting since it is so immediately relatable to practical, everyday life. Unlike, say, disciplines like physics or philosophy where you deconstruct nature's laws in retrospect, B-school studies are based on the man-made world and the impact of individual actions and choices. If I could place myself in the position of the individual making the choice, I could understand the analyses that went into the decision much better, I thought. With this radical insight, I approached classes with a new sense of purpose in the second term.

The first thing that my new approach taught me was to completely discredit all conclusions arrived at from market-research surveys. This burnt me badly. Every time I read an article like 'A study by the American Heart Research Institute proves that people who exercise live 50 per cent longer', I didn't take it at face value. As a result, I became fat, lazy and miserable, and blamed it on the IIM. After all, it was highly likely that stoned researchers, too lazy to exert themselves to collect real data, filled those data sheets themselves with a joint in one hand and a pen in the other. At least, that's what Sarkar and I did.

Our intentions were always pure, though. In selecting our project for the research in marketing methods, for example, we agonized long and hard over the topic to pick.

Sarkar said, 'Let's research cigarettes and what triggers smoking in college—peer pressure, chicks, stress relief, or something else. It will be fun to have a quantitative model to predict the likelihood of a college kid starting to smoke, based on his environment.'

Vinod had a different perspective. 'Bugger off, I'm not doing any smoking research. That will give you another reason to smoke your gaanja in the name of research. I want to do something that affects me more directly, and doesn't involve alcohol or drugs.'

We let a few more months pass in indecision until one day Vinod informed us that the project was due the next day. We had to come up with something, and Sarkar naturally assumed leadership.

'Samrat boy, remember what Goenka said in Dharamsala about how the self-centred pursuit of material ambition leads to restlessness and unhappiness? Well, IIM is all about that—better grades, foreign jobs, higher salaries, positions of power, etc. So why don't we measure whether the quest for these causes unhappiness? It could be profound. Everyone comes here chasing happiness but ends up getting further and further away from it.'

'Interesting,' I said. 'We could create a survey asking questions about the degree of happiness and contentment in people's lives. Measure the difference between B-school students and the population outside. And validate the hypothesis that business school screws you over.'

Vinod concurred. 'So you guys did learn something there. All I've heard are stories about hash and hippies.'

'So we have a plan,' Sarkar said. He proceeded to give out instructions. 'Vinod, why don't you type the report, assuming that our hypothesis is true? Let Samrat boy and me prepare the questionnaire and collect the data from students here and regular people in Bangalore. If the data doesn't validate the hypothesis, we will quickly change the conclusions.' Vinod left for the computer lab while we went to get the bike keys from Sarkar's room.

Once there, he rolled a joint at top speed and held it up asking, 'One for the road?' One became two, and then some more. He brought out a bottle of rum and some chilled Coke and we had a drink each of that as well.

'It is kind of humid and sticky outside today,'

Sarkar said. I laughed. I knew where this was going and didn't mind.

'Maybe we can just estimate the data ourselves. It would be quite accurate. After all, we were normal folks before we became abnormal B-school students,' Sarkar said.

'Not entirely inaccurate,' I agreed. 'Let's not tell Vinod though. He gets hyper about this kind of stuff.' So, passing around another joint, we completed two questionnaires and calculated the mean scores.

'We are not being dishonest,' Sarkar reassured me, although I didn't particularly need reassurance. 'We won't claim the base size was a hundred or anything. Maybe we can specify in font size one somewhere in the bibliography, which no one is going to read anyway, that the study was conducted on a base size of two.' A lazy couple of hours passed. We went to join Vinod in the lab where we ran the analyses on the means on the statistical software together.

'It's a near-perfect correlation; business school makes you unhappy!' Vinod exclaimed as the results came out. 'Wow, I think we have discovered something much bigger than ourselves here. We should ask the professor if these outcomes should be presented to the IIM board of directors. It could shape the way they think of the curriculum. How can they promote unhappiness?'

Sarkar and I exchanged worried glances. Stoned, we had probably steered too much towards our biases while filling in the questionnaire. Sarkar tried to dissuade Vinod gently. 'I think we need to validate it with more rigour in the sample collection and broaden the scope a bit.'

Broaden the scope from the already significant base size of two, that is, I thought.

Vinod's enthusiasm didn't dampen. 'No problem, we could position this as preliminary findings. No one is claiming this is the definitive answer. But it still merits sharing.'

It finally took a stroke of genius from me to prevent Vinod from broadcasting the results. 'You know, I think the basic methodology we used is flawed. We cannot prove conclusively that the IIM makes you unhappy for ever. The effect could be temporary. We should have designed a temporal, longitudinal study that covers people who have graduated from business school as well, if we really want to prove the hypothesis.' Sarkar looked at me in silent appreciation. Vinod was crushed but he knew I was right. We couldn't turn that around in a day, so we submitted the project as it was, while Vinod diligently called out this lapse in the executive summary. I was finally a real manager, I realized with pride. I could lie readily and effectively use jargon to stem the enthusiasm of everyone who worked with me.

I had another series of insights in a course called study of Indian society, generally dismissed by my classmates as a 'soft subject where you have to fart in the exams to do well'. After all, the coursework required no knowledge of complex mathematical insights or regression formulae—how dare someone waste time talking about worthless concepts like history, society and culture in business school?

For me though, the Indian society course represented a turning point in my understanding of India and provided one of the most definitive answers to the questions that had brought me here. The lectures covered India's social and cultural history and its impact in shaping the modern Indian psyche. Through the course, I understood, for example, that collectivism or relying on a network of familial and social connections is a uniquely Indian value, vastly different from the Western ethos of individualism and self-reliance. Being a hybrid of these Indian and Western values, I realized, was part of the reason for my social confusion. While my American colleagues were content to just hang out making small talk in a restaurant or bar on weekends, I had always sought deeper bonds and more meaningful conversation, a result perhaps of the weekend get-togethers with the circle of Indian friends that my parents had in Kentucky. In Manhattan, where these networks were in short supply, I had been besieged by loneliness. Contrarily, in India I screamed for personal space sometimes, just wanting to be left alone, read a book and think.

And somehow, I could never convey this politely to Sarkar and Vinod, defaulting several times into becoming an unwilling, morose companion in their well-intentioned plans.

Other aspects of Indian society that seemed buried in the past, like the caste system, also became clearer to me. A distorted form of that system is still very much a part of Indian attitudes, and it explained, for example, why Mom and Dad could never embrace the concept of 'dignity of labour'. They frowned upon every attempt I made to take up a summer job flipping burgers or as a newspaper delivery boy. ('Beta, these jobs are not for us.') Then, I had blamed them for not assimilating or allowing me to assimilate, but now I understood Mom and Dad better. They'd had a lifetime of social conditioning that a few years in the US couldn't change. Every day, I learnt something new in the course that helped me define myself better. It also made me realize that I was touching the tip of the iceberg. There was a deeper truth that I was tantalizingly close to understanding—a truth about my relationships and my identity—but I just wasn't spending enough time thinking about it. I needed to take a step back and reflect on the many different images of India that stared at me every day.

There was a lot I needed to change in the next semester, I thought, in the two-day break between the second and third semester, as Dad's words came back to haunt me: 'Business school won't care about plugging the holes in your soul, whatever they are. You will have to slowly, deliberately fill them yourself—don't expect India to do that for you automatically.'

I would do just that, I thought. I would follow the Vipaasana regime and meditate every day. I would travel more, and dive into cultural and spiritual India. I would spend time nurturing the budding relationships I had with Sarkar and Vinod. I knew fully well that these were the only memories I would retain—living, breathing images—once my time in India was over. All else would be forgotten—little more than snapshots in a family album meant to fade with the passage of time. I made plans, and then I made even more plans.

The road to hell is paved with good intentions, and mine finally translated into little more than more intense revelry. Trying to spend more time getting to know Sarkar invariably meant getting sucked into the wild, frenzied partying at the institute as overwrought, misfit students took a break from the relentless academic pressure to enjoy a night of dancing, drinking and experimenting with more potent stuff. One such night, we decided to take a break from the party circuit and have dinner in Bangalore city instead. One of Sarkar's engineer friends had left town and loaned him his second-hand Hyundai to drive. Sarkar was immensely proud of it ('I'm going to score in the backseat, you guys, wait and see!') and was perpetually offering to drive us to the city. We gave in finally, though Vinod seemed unusually perplexed that night.

'You all right, man?' Sarkar asked him. 'You haven't said a word all evening, and you actually left some chicken for us today. Usually we only get to pick the bones after you are done.'

Vinod wasn't amused. 'I just heard from Gateway Consulting that I will be posted in Singapore for my summer internship. This completely changes things. You know my views about leaving India. I really want to join the company, but am planning to let it go now and find something else.'

'I think you should let it go anyway,' said Sarkar. 'Why waste a precious summer doing a useless consultancy internship?'

We ignored him, as usual.

'That's being pretty close-minded, dude,' I said to Vinod. 'You can help with India's development, pimping in a whorehouse in Singapore, if you want. In fact, you can probably contribute more from there because you will be earning in dollars. What do you hope to achieve by physically being here in India?'

Sarkar came back into the conversation with a vengeance. 'Man, if I had a chance, I would get out of India in a flash. I hate this place; the same shit everywhere. I don't want to work here, with colleagues whose entire lives revolve around their next promotion, and listen to them whine about office politics and how the boss is taking credit for their work. I don't want to commute to work every day in hours-long traffic jams or have my balls crushed in the Virar fast local train. I don't want to end up socializing with office perverts who have *Playboy* in one hand and their dicks in another. It's just a bunch of crap, man.'

I was surprised at this unexpected outburst. Just what was wrong with him? When did he develop such strong views about living in India? Or was he just trying to be contrary as usual?

Vinod seemed to have heard Sarkar's diatribe before. He just ignored it and answered my question instead. 'Look, I'm no patriot. If I was a patriot, I would have stuck to the army. I'm just another... small-towner, as Sarkar calls half of the class anyway. My mother is here, my relatives are here, that matters more than anything else. I may make more money in Singapore, even contribute more. But what about the intangibles? What about the thousand uniquely Indian sights and sounds you hear every day—the milkman, the chai-wala, train platforms, traffic jams? Who will compensate for that? It's just the principle, yaar. I never, ever want to leave.'

'But...' I began, when Sarkar interrupted me.

'Look behind you,' he said urgently. 'The television.'

We turned to the small television in the dimly lit restaurant. A minor actor, whom I'd seen playing pivotal roles like the hero's brother's friend and the rapist villain's fifth henchman in Mom's Bollywood flicks, was being interviewed by a random news channel. He was crying. Literally, not figuratively, real tears. The usual crowd of onlookers, always abundant in India, had gathered around him offering their condolences (and trying to get into the frame of the camera).

'Do you know why that thespian of Indian cinema is crying?' Sarkar asked.

Vinod and I shook our heads. It seemed completely irrelevant to the discussion at hand, but it was such a ridiculous sight that I was curious.

'He was an extra in a Bollywood flick which missed getting the Oscar for the best technical editing—or some other equally inconsequential award like that, an award which no one in America even knows exists. But of course, losing out on that award has hurt our national pride,' Sarkar said.

'So?' I said.

'Waiter, boss, can you change the channel?' said Sarkar, not answering my question. The waiter flicked the switch. 'Look at that movie,' said Sarkar. A kitschy Hindi film was playing on the screen. An emaciated star son was showering his affection on a small-time actress by tearing her clothes apart. We looked at Sarkar quizzically.

'The film is produced and directed by the great showman of the Indian film industry, who pulls this wonderfully artistic stunt of making a special appearance in all his movies. Alfred Hitchcock is applauding him from his grave for his ingenuity,' Sarkar said witheringly.

'The point being?' said Vinod.

'We're just dying to get a little appreciation from *phoren*. America and Europe, the mother ships. A crummy award thrown at us by America is the ultimate nod to our national pride,' said Sarkar caustically. 'All our ideas come from the West, yet you talk about the "uniqueness" of India's sights and sounds.'

'Not everything is about your movies,' said Vinod sourly.

'Really?' said Sarkar. He pointed to a group of young guys sitting next to us, whose soft faces looked incongruous against their pierced ears and spiked hair. 'Then why do these jokers want to have "organic food only"—didn't you just hear them? Do they understand that one breath of the Bangalore air outside will neutralize a lifetime of organic meals? No. Angelina Jolie eats organic food, so Ramachandra wants organic food. Do they really enjoy listening to Coldplay songs on their iPod? Why does Erich Segal's *Love Story* sell more than Pran's *Chacha Chaudhary* comics? Are they going to meet twenty-five-year-old Jenny from New York when Mommy has already arranged a marriage with nineteen-year-old Lovleen from Bhatinda? Why are we celebrating Thanksgiving, Mother's Day and now even Halloween for God's sake?'

'Can you keep your voice down?' I asked. 'They aren't deaf.'

'Your thesis on pop culture is very enlightening,' said Vinod. 'But that means nothing in my context. I just like it here man, simple. Not everything in life has to be an anthropological study.'

Sarkar piped down a bit. 'Whatever,' he said. 'Your hell.'

'I do think you should give it a try, though,' I said, trying to bring back some rationality to the argument. 'It's just a two-month corporate internship. You aren't signing off to become somebody's girlfriend in the Singapore Alcatraz.'

'It's not an internship thing, boss,' Vinod said. 'What if the Singapore office gives me a pre-placement offer? What then? Then you will say, "Work there for just two more years and get some work experience". And then, "Just wait till you are married so your wife can experience living in a different country", followed by "Wait till you have kids, they can be Singapore citizens". And before you know it, your whole life has been spent pining for permanence, belonging neither here nor there.' He drained his whiskey and asked the waiter for a refill.

He had a point. Rather uncomfortably, it reminded me of Dad. Wouldn't he have been happier if he had never chosen to move to the US? His friends back home were happier, he had said in occasional unguarded moments, they had friends and family around them.

'Look,' said Vinod, sensing perhaps that he had touched a raw nerve. 'Let's skip this topic. We won't get anywhere. In fact, let's just shut up and drink for a while.'

'And enjoy this uplifting music?' said Sarkar.

We laughed. The place topped the list of the most depressing places I had been to. A badly lit tube-light cast a dark, gloomy shadow on the untidily arranged tables in the room. The tablecloths were tattered or stained, and the only others there were the six wannabe rockers at the adjoining table, whose artistic and cultural tastes had already been dissected in detail by Sarkar. Bad disco music blared from the stereo system.

'Remind me again, why are we here?' I said.

'Because I'm not a banker,' smiled Vinod. 'I spent the last rupee of my army savings on the Rajasthan trip. Nowhere in Bangalore, not even in a dhaba, can you find drinks this cheap.'

'I'm here for the organic food,' quipped Sarkar.

We steadily worked our way through multi-hued bottles of rum and whiskey. My head throbbed from the mix. I needed to stop, I thought, when Sarkar held out a drink he'd mixed for me.

'Try this one. It gives you the ultimate kick. In

villages and small towns all over India, where there is no money to spare on fancy addictions, they mix cheap whiskey with beer for an immediate rush. You are out after just a glass. Bloody efficient.' Trust Sarkar to know this.

I took a tentative sip. It was surprisingly sweet and tasty. I drained the glass and took another. The music suddenly changed to a Sufi number. The DJ at the ramshackle establishment seemed to have chosen this night to find a piece of his soul as well.

'Enjoy the song while it lasts,' said Sarkar. 'Soon,' he pointed to the group next to us, 'one of them will get up and ask the DJ-cum-cook-cum-janitor to play Bryan Adams's *Best Days of My Life*. They will all hug each other after that—fancy an American song they can actually understand!'

'So?' said Vinod, sounding irritated at Sarkar's unrelenting cynicism. 'Some people are happy and want to celebrate. Not everybody has had a troubled…' He stopped. 'Whatever.'

A look passed between Sarkar and Vinod. In that moment, I realized they knew things about each other that I didn't know, and perhaps would never know. My last conscious feeling before things became completely hazy was a stab of envy at what they shared, and how incapable I was of giving myself so completely to….

❉

The next thing I can recall clearly about that night is sitting in the dark in a fifteen-by-ten prison cell with at least a dozen starving men. My head hurt so much that I wished I could die. Some fresh air would have helped, but all there was to inhale was the stench of broken toilets. Rats scurried about on the floor, which was splattered with a yellow liquid that I was sure was fresh vomit.

I was told later that I had been so far gone after the lethal whiskey-and-beer cocktail that by the time Sarkar suggested a drive in his friend's car—'Let's go have an ice cream and tea, man'—Vinod had to pretty much carry me to the car. Once there, I had suddenly recovered and fought them hard to sit on the hood. Disjointed bits of conversation came back to me.

Vinod: 'Mr America, have you gone nuts? This is a potholed Bangalore road, not America's smooth highways. One bump and you are gone forever.'

Sarkar: 'Let it be, man, he won't fall off. Physics will save him: since the car has a forward momentum he will be pushed backward, and can't lose his balance. It's the ultimate poor man's Leonardo DiCaprio king-of-the-world, wind-blowing-against-your-face kick—even if this is a second-hand Hyundai and not the *Titanic*. I have done it many times at IIT.'

Vinod: 'Okay, fine, if you know the science and stuff, which I don't of course.'

More recollections: the cool, sharp sensation of the air on my face and the sudden realization—I was on the fucking hood! Loud thumping on the hood to make Sarkar stop. And is that a roadblock coming up ahead? Louder thumping till the car stops. Two cops with beedis, startled in their slack time. Sudden desire to puke. Retching in front of the cops. Quick breath analyser test with some complex contraption. Shocked, stunned faces, how can someone's blood alcohol be so high? Another sudden realization: I was likely fucked!

My memory starts to get clearer from there. Sarkar gets out of the car confidently and addresses the cops in hail-fellow-well-met fashion. 'Sir, don't trouble him. He's just a kid who has come from foreign land. How much do you want?' Knowing smiles are exchanged. 'Just some chai paani, we know you are college kids. Even we have college-going children, these things happen,' one cop says, smiling. Things are settled at the princely sum of Rs 500 each.

The money is about to change hands and we are ready to go, all smiles, just another happy picture for the IIM scrapbook, when all hell breaks loose. A marked police car stops at the roadblock and a senior police official steps out. An immediate, perceptible shift occurs in everybody's reactions. The police constables distance themselves from us—money hasn't changed hands yet and they are innocent. They turn harsh and accusatory all of a sudden.

'Sir,' they tell the officer, pointing to me, 'just look at his blood-alcohol level. Unbelievable! These kids nowadays, sir, they need to be taught a lesson.'

Sarkar's eyes are flashing with excitement. Crazy bastard. A paper bag filled with grass is lying arrogantly unconcealed on the front seat of our car. Vinod gets out and shows his ex-military identification card. I retch again at the wrong time in the wrong place—right on the inspector's boots.

'Sir,' the senior official addresses Vinod respectfully, 'what are you doing with these lowlifes? I respect you, sir, please go home now. Let me deal with them.'

Vinod refuses to listen. 'These are my friends. Our sincere apologies, inspector. We were just having a bit of harmless fun and things got out of hand. Please forgive us.'

The official turns out to be a decorated inspector of the Bangalore police, given to surprise checks to fix the rampant police corruption and drunken driving. Luck is well and truly against us. His eyes fall on the bag on the front seat. He goes over, tears it open and smells it. 'Bloody youngsters!' he says in disgust, 'bloody spoiled youngsters.' He means Sarkar and me. Vinod has been absolved, of course. 'Take them to the police station,' he orders the constables. What? Did I hear him correctly? It's marijuana, for heaven's sake, it's legal in a few countries and a medical curative used in hospitals nearly everywhere else. Are you doing this because I puked on your nicely polished shiny shoes? Unfortunately, no words come out. Just more vomit. This time I target it away from his shoes but it doesn't help.

'Just take these two away, will you?' he barks out to the constables.

Turning to Vinod, he says politely, 'Sir, why don't you take the car and leave?'

But Vinod accompanies us, much to the inspector's discomfiture. Sarkar remains crazily calm as we're shunted inside the police van. I'm too hammered to think straight, but I know we're in a lot of trouble. At the station, the constables, who haven't said a word to us in the van, take us to the officer on duty.

'Tyagi Sir has asked you to take care of these two,' one of them says, pointing to Sarkar and me. Vinod looks worried then, and establishes his credentials again. He convinces the officer not to file a case and let him make a couple of calls while Sarkar and I are led to the lockup.

By now, I am fully in my senses and so is Sarkar, though the bastard still looks okay, almost as though he's enjoying the adventure. I have horrifying thoughts of being sodomized in the cell. Wasn't everyone raped in prisons? Fuck, fuck, fuck! I'm almost in tears. Fear of enclosed spaces. *The Count of Monte Cristo*, Alcatraz, *The Shawshank Redemption*—all of it flashes through my mind to form bone-chilling, terrifying visions of sexual assault and murder.

Sarkar's voice cuts through the darkness. 'Try this one. I removed the filter,' he says as he holds out a joint.

I reach out for it involuntarily when the reality of the situation strikes me with a crushing, almost physical force. The intense panic of the last few hours finally catches up with me. I start to sob with my hand over my mouth, for fear of waking up someone. But I'm having a full-blown panic attack and can't stop shaking. The thin, starving man curled up by my feet wakes up and looks at me irritably. He scratches his fierce, pockmarked face.

'Abe chikne, naya hai kya? Will you shut up or should I make you shut up?' he growls, then yawns, releasing a cloud of foul-smelling breath in my direction before turning around and going back to sleep.

Chikne, doesn't that mean faggot?

Oh God, no, not this. You can't turn my life into a prison fuck-fest! I weep openly now.

'Have you gone nuts?' Sarkar looks at me, wide-eyed with surprise. 'What are you crying about?' I stare at him and the joint in his hand in disbelief.

I could kill him. My head is spinning with what I'd like to scream out at him. But all I manage is an angry whisper, 'Oh man, you're the one that's nuts! What are you so happy about? We are screwed,

royally screwed. How long are we going to be here?
Are we both going to be raped and murdered here?
What is wrong with you? Don't you realize the shit
we are in? I can't believe this!' I run my hand through
my hair frantically. How many years of prison do you
get for being caught with marijuana? A few hours
ago we were role-playing CEOs in an organization
process design class in an air-conditioned classroom
in business school. A few months ago, I was on the
fiftieth floor of a swanky office which overlooked
the Hudson river. What the hell happened? It's
over, my future has ended even before it started.

Sarkar whispers back, 'Please grow up. We're
here for an hour at the most. Vinod is going to call
my father if I'm not mistaken and things will be
fine soon.'

I am stunned at his foolishness. 'Your father is a
businessman. This isn't about money, Sarkar, we have
committed a federal offence, or whatever you call it in
India. A senior police inspector has caught us with a
carload of marijuana in our possession and he is out
to screw us. What will it take for you to realize we
are screwed? Our careers end here. Business school
is over. Your big talk doesn't work any more. Man, I
can't believe I let you convince me all these months
that Rs 500 solves everything in India.'

'If you're so worried, you can tell them you had
nothing to do with it,' Sarkar says. 'I'll tell them it's
all mine if it comes down to it.'

I'm so angry I can explode. 'Do you think I'd ever do that?' I almost forget to whisper. 'This isn't a rerun of *Law and Order*, or whatever crappy show you get your foolish ideas about America from. I don't rat on friends. After all we've been through, is that all you think of me?'

Sarkar keeps quiet. I start to cry again. Mom and Dad, what do I tell you? Where did I go so wrong? I regretted that cursed moment when I decided to come to India. Oh Christine, your chance comment screwed me over.

Fifteen minutes later, the cell door opens. Interrogation, I think—done, fucked. The same constable who had locked us in escorts us outside. 'Sir, will you have some tea? We are very, very sorry, sir. Please forgive us. It was Inspector Tyagi who told us to... What could we do, sir? I have young children at home, sir.' He almost dies 'sir-ing' us.

I can't believe it. What just happened? We are treated like royalty from here on. We are served tea, biscuits and even piping hot omelette and toast. The duty inspector gets up to offer us his seat. Our abandoned car appears parked right outside the station under the 'No Parking' sign where even the police can't park their jeeps. Even Inspector Tyagi calls to speak to Sarkar to apologize. Police officers hang around obsequiously, fawning on every word we utter. I stare in awe.

'Not a word to the media or the IIM,' Sarkar says

to the police officials, acting like a bloody inspector-general of police briefing his subordinates.

'Of course, Sarkar sir. How can you even think that way? You're like our son, sir.'

We get out. Sarkar drives the car again—this time I elect not to sit on the hood. I don't think I'll ever sit on the hood of a car again.

※

Vinod took the wheel of the car as I sank into the back seat. The air was thick with tension.

'That was very selfish of you,' said Vinod, breaking the silence.

'Selfish? Me?' said Sarkar. 'I saved you guys.'

'I'm not talking about that,' said Vinod.

Sarkar kept quiet.

'The moment you run into trouble, you call him, don't you? Then you forget all the "Oh, I'm this fucked-up poor little rich boy. I had such a difficult childhood" bull,' said Vinod. 'That's where all your false bravado comes from, doesn't it? You know Daddy dearest is going to bail you out if it comes to that.'

'Don't speak about things you don't understand. Not everything is as linear as it is in the army,' said Sarkar.

'Why don't I understand? Just because I don't have a father?' said Vinod. 'I've seen enough of the world to know that you're no Hamlet. There is no

Shakespearean tragedy in your life. Do you know what your problem is? Besides the fact that you don't want to grow up?'

Sarkar didn't express any interest in Vinod's diagnosis.

'You hate being in his shadow. I spoke to him today, and I know when I hear genuine concern. If he didn't care about anyone but himself, as you claim, why would he stop everything to make those calls today?' Vinod said.

'He's worried about his reputation.'

'Like hell he is. Every day there is a failed celebrity son doing something stupid to get attention—just like you. Does anyone care about Puru Raj Kumar or Fardeen Khan or any of those other idiots who are caught snorting cocaine or slitting their wrists?'

'You seem to be quite the psychologist,' said Sarkar stiffly. 'Is Dr Phil taking lessons for the Indian Army now or what? Why don't you share your theory on Barkha Dutt's couch instead of shooting off here?'

Vinod looked as if he was ready to explode.

'Care to throw a few words of explanation my way?' I said from the back of the car.

A brief silence followed.

'Just keep it to yourself, okay?' Sarkar said finally. 'I am Byomkesh Sarkar's son.'

The name sounded familiar. Oh no, it couldn't be. The brilliant Richard Branson-ish, charismatic

Indian serial entrepreneur who launched new
ventures with the same speed as he changed the
bikini models by his side. So this was where it
came from—the sharp intelligence, the natural
aptitude for numbers, the disdain for authority
and the natural leadership abilities. Also explained
why Shine Sarkar was conspicuously absent when
Byomkesh Sarkar visited the IIM campus for a
lecture on entrepreneurship in his trademark flashy
private jet. Come to think of it, Byomkesh had even
alluded to feeling a 'special connection' with the IIM,
which I had mistaken for the usual let's-all-feel-
good-about-ourselves speech. I didn't even know he
was married, he always had the latest number by
his side—which was perhaps the real reason why we
had got in this mess today.

'Have you ever discussed anything with *him*?' said
Vinod. 'Maybe it was your mother's fault, maybe she
left him, maybe she had an affair. Who knows?'

'Again, don't speak without...' began Sarkar. But
I cut him off. I had more important questions on
my mind.

'Why didn't you tell me before?' I asked.

Both of them fell silent.

'It didn't seem important,' said Sarkar.

'Important enough to tell Vinod, though,' I said.

Another long silence.

'Look, it's not all my fault,' said Sarkar eventually.

'When is it ever your fault?' I said testily.

'Well, you always seem so... so self-involved. Don't get me wrong. I know you care about me, us, Vinod and I, that is. But you always seem so caught up in your own problems, you just don't seem interested in anything else,' he said.

Vinod didn't contradict Sarkar for the first time that night. It hurt.

We drove in silence the rest of the way and reached the campus late in the night.

'Tea?' said Sarkar tentatively.

'I'll pass,' I said. 'I'm heading to my room.'

'Look, I'm sorry. I didn't mean what I said. It's been a crazy day, even for us,' said Sarkar.

I knew he had meant exactly what he'd said.

'No, it isn't that. I think I just need to do my own thing for a while,' I said.

Was I really so self-centred, I thought, as I walked back to my room. Maybe I was just going through a 'phase', a convenient word that explained most irresponsible behaviour. Or maybe the reality was much simpler. I had led a privileged life. Unlike Vinod, I hadn't ever had to take care of a widowed mother and a younger sister, financially or emotionally. Unlike Sarkar, I never had a troubled relationship with my parents, real or imagined. I had never been forced to think of a cause greater than myself, perhaps that's why I remained so completely immersed in myself. Sarkar and Vinod had been right when they, like Dad, had called me 'soft and self-centred', even if not in as many words. Every day, I saw Sarkar sink farther and farther into an abyss, but I had never held out a hand to him. Why then did I expect him to unburden himself to me?

As usual, though, running away was so much easier than confronting the problem. For the rest of the semester, I buried my nose in my books and kept away from parties, drinking, dope—and Sarkar and Vinod. In less than a month, I'd have to report at the Shivam Chemicals head office in Mumbai for my summer internship, and I couldn't wait for it to start. Or rather, I couldn't wait for the semester to end. A year ago, if someone had said that I would be dying to peddle shampoos and sanitary napkins in rural India by the end of the year, I would have looked at them and wondered whether like me, they too were losing their minds in Manhattan.

But here I was—anxiously awaiting the end of my torturous first year at business school and the beginning of my internship, selling soap in the hinterlands of India.

10

Selling Soap to Raja Bhaiya in Benares

April 1, 2001, half past ten in the morning, and I found myself battling sleep as usual, not in class this time but in the plush corporate offices of Shivam Chemicals in Mumbai. I had come straight from Bangalore after a curt end-of-term farewell to Sarkar and Vinod and felt too drained to show any sign of warmth to the thirty-odd summer interns from other top B-schools across India. In any case, a cursory glance indicated that there were no interesting female prospects, and lots of bright-eyed engineer-looking guys. Clearly, lack of diversity and chronic overenthusiasm were afflictions that dogged all the B-schools in India.

The perfunctory introductions were made with the usual cute ice-breaking exercise led by human resources that mostly serves the purpose of making people even more uncomfortable than they are, thereby, logically, freezing the ice completely. The question this time was, 'If you could choose, what animal would you like to be and why?' I began to doze off as the usual, predictable B-school stuff followed ('a dog because I'm loyal', 'a swallow because I love to fly fast and high', 'an eagle because I'm always focused on the target') before Manu, the balding, serious-looking dude next to me, said, 'I would like to be Pamela Anderson's lap-dog because… because… do I really need to say why?'

I sat up in my chair. Well done, my friend, that sets the bar, I laughed silently as the others tried to mask their astonishment at his brazenness with polite titters. The suits from Shivam looked at each other uncomfortably before they too broke into polite, embarrassed smiles. I was next, and taking a cue from Manu, said, 'A cow, I love the way they stand stoned all day doing nothing in the fields.' More snickers. A bunch of harmless ones later, Murali, a long-haired guy who looked pretty stoned to me, drawled, 'Don't want to be an animal, don't like them.' From anyone else it would have appeared banal. From this guy with his lazy, 'fuck you' tone and rock-star hair, it was actually funny and quite a few of us burst out laughing. This was getting to be fun. I felt the last few days at the IIM draining away from me.

The human resources manager, an eager-to-please young woman, was a bit frazzled by the sudden turn her harmless exercise had taken. She tried to get the proceedings back in control.

Of course, what better way to get a B-school gathering in control than to harmlessly drop the 'C' word: careers? It is no secret that IIM students live and breathe for placements, and nothing, absolutely nothing, not even descriptions of the kinkiest, smuttiest sexual acts, could get their attention like talk about a Pre-Placement Offer (PPO), job offers made to a select few interns immediately after their internship. Shivam Chemicals was one of the best companies on campus and getting an offer from them would have made the years of bonded labour that led to business school worth it. Everybody strained to listen.

Her talk was appropriately vague and full of the usual management bull: 'All thirty of you are from the best business schools in the country. You are all brilliant, and I would like everyone to give themselves a hand for doing so well in your chosen fields.'

I hated this everyone-gets-a-trophy-in-summer-camp kind of crap and didn't think it merited an acknowledgment. Over-eager jobseekers clapped hard, though. Every action was vital now, the suits could be judging every move.

'Shivam Chemicals will be privileged to welcome some of you back into our offices after summer internship. But, (there is always a 'but', I thought), please don't consider it a reflection of your competence if you are not extended an offer. Maybe there wasn't a cultural fit.'

I could never understand this 'culture fit' stuff. For me, it was just a polite way of saying, 'Tough shit.

You are just not good enough to work here.' I mean there were so many 'cultures' —there were 'cultures' of companies, 'subcultures' of departments within companies and even 'sub-subcultures' of functions within departments. So which culture were you supposed to fit into? And why didn't people ever talk about not fitting into the 'culture' of the IIM? Maybe I was much more damned competent than Chetan or even Sarkar, but just didn't fit into the 'culture'. That's why I was so miserably fucked there. How about that?

She droned on before bald Manu cut her short. 'Just how many offers are you planning to give this year? Simply speaking, how many of us will get an offer?'

She was expecting that question. More drivel: 'Shivam Chemicals is not committed to a defined number. We will evaluate each candidate as an individual, and if there is a strong cultural fit we would like to invite you back to grow the legacy of this company.'

Oh please, spare us this. Couldn't you have at least come up with a marginally honest answer? I raised my hand.

'Does that mean all thirty of us can get an offer if we fit into Shivam's culture?'

She stumbled on that one, knowing that the politically correct answer was 'Yes', but saying that would make her come across as an idiot.

A dapper, suave-looking suit, who had earlier introduced himself as the head of Shivam's laundry business, bailed her out. 'Look, let's be realistic here. I'm sure you guys know that every year we give no more than five offers after internship. This year is no different. Maybe four offers, maybe five or even six, but it is going to be in that vicinity.'

Silence greeted that statement. I could see other minds churning like mine. Being in the top five among thirty interns was equivalent to being in the top twenty per cent or so of this collection of overachievers. In business school, I wasn't even in the top fifty per cent of the class, and this was a selection of thirty of the brightest and smartest across the IIMs. Unless success in Indian corporations was based on entirely different factors from success in B-school, I was going back without a pre-placement offer from my internship. As if I cared, I thought, did I really need to collect another meaningless job offer to find meaning in my life? Something caught my eye. I looked to my side to see Murali, the rocker dude, dozing off. He had slept through the information session. I liked him immediately.

The discussion immediately caused a perceptible shift in the mood and the familiar B-school testosterone came into play again. Everything went downward from there. Week One of summer internship is usually a time for catching up on your sleep, forging new connections and wining and dining on the company's expense before you are packed off to lonely outposts in the hinterlands. There would be big-picture orientation presentations about the company, which even less hardened cynics than me wouldn't care about. Why care who your CEO in the German headquarters was (and which nubile secretary's pants he is trying to get into, Murali added) when you are a lowly summer intern making photocopies in rural India? But trust overambitious B-school freshmen to ruin this idyllic period. Every speaker in the orientation was assailed by questions, each question meant to demonstrate the superiority of the questioner, each questioner trying his or her hardest to grab every spare point available towards the goal of getting a job offer—which didn't even exist yet.

Bloody irrational, I thought, increasingly irritated by the interminable questions, didn't they realize the internship assignments don't begin until next week? Who is going to give them a job offer for asking for details about the company's expense-report filing system? Be nice, I chided myself immediately, don't be self-centred. Unlike you, these folks have worked hard to get here, not everyone is born with a silver spoon up his ass. But the relentless volleys of questions about each and every strategy of the company, its many operating units, its profit and loss statements, even its office facilities and mail-rooms, broke my resolve to be nice. I felt more like a misfit than ever, finding myself in the middle again: neither as cool as Murali who slept shamelessly through the session, nor halfway as ambitious as the rest.

Finally, it was time for the last session of the day, an overview of the security systems in the corporate headquarters. Very basic, idiot-proof stuff—'This is your visitor's badge. This is where you buzz into the building. This is how the door opens. This is how you get out.' The chief of security leading the session had a jaded, lazy air about him. Left to his own, he would probably say, 'Look, these bastards at Shivam Chemicals shouldn't worry a flying fuck about security. They aren't producing nuclear weapons, they are making detergents and toilet soap. Not like the ISI or the CIA will steal their highly confidential bleach formulas. So my humble advice to you is to sleep through this stupid session. Please don't make it any more painful for me than it already is.' He probably couldn't say what he really thought about the session, though. So he launched into a detached, uninspired monologue and ended mechanically with, 'Any questions?' He didn't seem to expect or encourage any questions, though.

Yes, I have one question, I thought, can you please tell me where I can score some marijuana in Mumbai? You see, I have kind of broken up with Shine Sarkar, my usual source, although that sounds terribly gay and melodramatic. Anyway, he is in London doing a useless banking internship. But I desperately need a couple of joints for the next few days if I have to survive the orientation. Can you help with that, please?

Instead of me asking about things that really mattered, a bespectacled, overenthusiastic fellow intern asked a question in his cocksure baritone. 'What about tailgating? That is, if someone follows me when I go in after buzzing my access card? How do you prevent that?'

I knew that bastard had an answer up his sleeve as he smirked when the mild-mannered chief of security, who seemed surprised that anyone was paying any attention to him, stumbled through the answer. The intern looked at the HR manager to ensure his point was being registered. 'Well, I have read that companies in the US have now installed new radars which beep immediately if more than one person enters with the same access card. Maybe we should consider installing that at Shivam. Corporate security is such an important issue, after all,' he said smugly.

The poor security chief stared nonplussed. I could have gladly wrung the intern's neck for being such a bastard. I did the next best thing. I jumped in with my first comment of the day. 'Actually, they have proven not to work. Goldman Sachs, my ex-employer on Wall Street, was the first company to use them, but they figured that the cost of continuous monitoring every alarm outweighs its advantages. Especially since security breaches rarely occur during office hours.'

There, that settled the bastard, I thought. I had totally made this up, but my American accent made me the last word on corporate America. The intern's face fell. I felt elated at my small-minded meanness. My day suddenly became brighter and happier, although there was still the social hour to go.

As soon as we moved to the club room, the location for the party, Murali, the long-haired rocker dude, walked over and high-fived me. '*Jigar*, that was the best comment of the day by far.' He grabbed a drink from the bar. '*Jigar*, what will you have?' he asked. My post-prison resolve to avoid alcohol dissolved. Hell, what harm could a beer do? And I badly needed one to get through the social hour. I succumbed.

Murali turned out to be quite chatty and shared my annoyance at the others. 'When will these bastards learn?' he said, pointing to a group of interns who were trying to cosy up to the top suits. 'They have been going on since morning, and internship hasn't even officially begun yet. Thankfully, I didn't have to tolerate this nonsense at my school.'

I was surprised. 'Didn't you guys have to attend classes there? Weren't there grades for class-participation?'

Murali shook his head. '*Jigar*, we didn't have compulsory attendance. I attended only those classes where professors discourage irrelevant questions. Like the statistics professor. First day of class, instead of the usual "There are no bad questions, all questions are good questions" crap, he said, "There are smart questions and there are stupid questions. Please don't advertise your stupidity and limit your stupid questions during class time so you are respectful of everyone's time."

'I loved him immediately. There was silence, and then some smartass asked, "How do we judge without asking, which question is good and which is stupid, sir?" Do you know what the prof said? "This is exactly the kind of stupid question I was referring to. Please avoid asking such questions in class and ask me later instead." Man, that was priceless. *Jigar*, I attended every class after that.'

I wished I had gone to his school instead. No compulsory attendance would have solved at least some of my problems. As we got progressively drunk, we swapped more stories from our respective campuses, our laughter getting more boisterous by the moment. With a pang, I realized I missed Sarkar and Vinod. I wished I hadn't acted like such an ass the last month. I made up my mind to get out and give both of them a call when Manu, the bald dude, joined us.

'Those fuckers are kissing the foreigner's asses now, as if they'll all get offers in New York and London after speaking to them for two minutes,' he said witheringly, looking towards the interns who were chatting up the CEO's American and European entourage.

We continued about how screwed up the IIM system was and what a bunch of idiots our fellow interns were. Not a single positive, meaningful thought was shared through the evening. There was no need—we were friends for a week and then we would move on, probably never to meet again. None of us was seeking a deeper bond than that, and we revelled in our shallow cynicism.

The international biggies must have been bored of the ceaseless career probing ('What is the fast-track path to becoming the CEO?', 'How quickly can I get promoted?''How many years does it take to become general manager' etc.) because they started drifting towards our rowdy corner. By then, we were drunk enough to ignore the fact that they were all big-shot directors from the 'global offices' of the company. Another unique Indian term, I thought. Every white foreigner, irrespective of whether he or she is Caucasian, Australian, Irish or Israeli, belongs to the 'global office', which is spoken about in hushed tones of awe and deference. He could be a janitor there for all they cared as long as he came from the 'global office'.

Murali and Manu paid no such obeisance to the global officers, instead lambasting the unsuspecting foreign directors for corporate malpractices and racism. '*Jigar*, I can't understand why Shivam Chemicals pay so much lip service to respecting diversity and being a true multinational. We don't even have an Indian running the Indian operations of the company, leave alone an Indian in a high position at the company's global headquarters,' Murali said.

I squirmed, wishing he would shut up. But Manu picked up. 'I agree. It's going to take another fifty years for Westerners to realize that Indians are not just call-centre operators who help fix toilets and ovens, but can actually manage companies pretty well.'

'Harvard and Wharton are crap,' said Murali irrelevantly. 'Do you know statistically it's about a hundred times more difficult to get into the IIM?' He thumped his chest, literally and figuratively. '*Jigar*. We have suffered.'

Indeed, I thought, his suffering was as apparent as the blue colour of the Cosmopolitan in his hand. I sank further in my seat. I knew they were talking nonsense and just trying to be provocative. But the crew of foreigners listened with rapt attention. More drunkenness and random cries of '*Desi* rocks!'

Anne, director of the company's huge soap business in France, finally asked, 'What is "*desi*"? I keep hearing that word from you guys.'

Murali elected to reply. '*Jigar*. It's a term Indians used to describe themselves, sometimes affectionately, but mostly derogatively. You know why we use it derogatively?' He was itching to answer yet another unasked question. 'It is because Indians are the biggest racists. We hate each other—north Indians hate south Indians, Bengalis hate Punjabis, resident Indians hate non-resident Indians, upper castes hate lower castes, Marwaris hate Parsis, Hindus hate Muslims, everyone hates everyone, but we all cohabit and together blame the West for racism.' That made no sense at all since he had just blamed the global officers for being white supremacists and discriminating against Indians.

The conversation then drifted to poverty, illiteracy, imperialist exploitation and the conspiracy against India, with Murali and Manu alternately blaming Britain and the US, and suddenly Pakistan, for all the country's troubles. To their credit, the directors took no offence at all. The party finally disbanded in the wee hours of the morning and we made our way to our rooms in the elegant hotel where the company had graciously put us up.

Murali, totally hammered by now, hugged me before stumbling to his room. 'You are the best man. *Jigar*. You are game for everything, always.' It reminded me of something Sarkar had once said, and I knew there was a principle here somewhere, but by then I was too smashed to figure it out.

I glanced in the giant mirror in my room and noticed my bloodshot eyes. I abstractly wondered whether I was developing a drinking problem. I decided to reflect on it over a beer from the mini-bar. It was pretty weak, so I decided to have two. I really didn't have a problem yet, I eventually decided over a shot of the delicious Jamaican rum they had stocked up in the refrigerator. True alcoholics probably never mixed their drinks. If they were addicts, they would probably like to get high on the same stuff every time, wouldn't they? I felt relieved and poured some Scotch in my glass in celebration, and didn't realize when I finally passed out on the sofa.

The rest of the week passed without incident—tepid orientation lectures, drunken evenings, hung-over mornings, apologetic phone calls to Vinod and Sarkar, broken promises to myself to be less self-centred and judgemental. Soon, I would be heading to Benares for the internship, to run the Shivam Chemicals sales team for the region. I had tried to find out more about what 'running' a sales team in India meant, chiefly what I was supposed to do there, but nobody could give me any clear answers. I realized this wasn't going to be anything like the structured investment banking internships I was used to. There would be no action plans, projects or deliverables—it was the Wild, Wild West out there. The only certainty was that there was a sales number to hit every month for Shivam's entire product line-up—soaps, detergents, shampoos, toilet goods, perfumes, deodorants, sanitary napkins—and it was left to you to achieve that. You could watch porn all day in the company's guest house or you could be out in the mean streets peddling your goods from morning to night. No one would know or care as long as you hit your month-end sales target.

Hoping I would have some company in Benares, I had asked Murali where he would be based. 'Hey man, I got lucky. I'm being sent to Bangalore to handle the company's foray into iced tea. *Jigar*. Couldn't have asked for anything better. You must tell me about all your local hangouts in Bangalore. What about you, what did you get? Delhi?'

When I told him where I was headed, Murali went ballistic. 'Benares! Ha ha! You'll be so fucked, man, just wait and see. It's the world's dirtiest, most miserably crowded city. Hey, Manu, he is going to Benares, yaar. How like these idiots to send the only foreigner in the batch to Benares while the rest of us go to big cities. *Jigar*!'

I called up Mom and Dad.

'Beta, when will this foolishness end?' Dad said. 'We didn't raise you to spend your life lying on the ghats of Benares. Soon all the privileges you take for granted will go away, you know. Goldman Sachs won't want you back, and you know how Wall Street is—once Goldman drops you, no one will want you. Stop chasing your ghosts all over India. You can still come back now if you want.'

I called up Sarkar and Vinod. Sarkar said it would be lawless and violent. 'Be careful there. Those bastards, they can steal your dick and you won't even realize it is missing.' He didn't care to explain who 'those bastards' were. Armed with these optimistic, encouraging words of wisdom I made my way to Benares with half a mind to buy a one-way ticket to Manhattan instead.

※

I needn't have worried. Despite being crowded and anarchic, or perhaps because of it, Benares turned out to be the quintessential Indian experience, full of contradictions that I had in mind when I left the safe environs of Manhattan. I lived alone in a bedroom at the nondescript company guest house, but found solace in the teeming crowds of pigs and pedestrians that abounded in the busy street outside. I vowed to read ancient Hindu philosophical and mythological texts, but defaulted to reading *Letters from the Penthouse* when the Upanishads became too much to crack. I enjoyed the absolute, perfect isolation of living in a city where I knew no one and no one knew me, but sought refuge in writing long, elaborate letters to Mom and Dad, Vinod, Sarkar and Peter. I jogged odd times in the day and night, sometimes to avoid the crowds, and sometimes to catch them at their most crowded.

I spent many evenings watching the daily aarti on the banks, mesmerized by the lights cast by the thousands of lamps on the water and the sound of devotional songs sung by impassioned devotees. They have so little, I thought every time I heard them, yet they have so much to thank God about. And here I am, a rich, fat, selfish bastard who has everything but can't stop complaining. Everything but happiness, I would remind myself. But what is happiness, and why does it continue to mock me? I have never been a religious person but the mystical aartis did rouse something in me, and I desperately wanted to believe in the existence of a higher truth than the one I knew.

The banks of the Ganga provided their fair share of bizarre experiences as well. One night as I sat staring transfixed at a funeral pyre long after the crowds had dispersed for the night, I heard a sudden movement from the pyre. Benares has a reputation for being a dangerous city at night, and Vinod had forewarned me that taking midnight strolls on the ghats was begging for trouble. But I'd smoked some strong stuff and was acutely lethargic. The abrupt movement which had attracted my attention seemed to be caused by a thin, white ghost emerging from somewhere around the pyre. His tall, angular body was covered with ash, and he seemed to be gliding towards me. I wondered briefly whether I was hallucinating because of the marijuana, but quickly dismissed the possibility—I had smoked way more before.

He stood beside me now. 'Do you have a cigarette?' he asked in perfect English, with a trace of an American accent. Clearly, he sounded more like a man than a ghost. But then, how does one know how ghosts sound, I thought? My heartbeat returned to normal, though, as I looked closely. It was a breed I recognized well—an American pothead hoping unsuccessfully to discover missing pieces of his soul in India. I saw one in the mirror every day, after all. I offered him my new favourite cigarette brand, India Kings.

'Ah, I like it,' he said after taking a small puff. We kept silent for a while—what small talk do you make with an ash-smeared white American yogi who just appeared out of a funeral pyre? 'Where are you from?' he said finally. Uh-huh. For me this wasn't the easiest conversation starter. I decided to stick to Manhattan for this conversation.

'Well, then we are from the same country,' he said. 'I was born in Texas, and even worked as an investment banker in Manhattan for a while. Great city. I tried to have a bite off the Big Apple, but I guess I couldn't digest it.' I looked to see if he was pulling my leg but he seemed serious. I wondered if I would become like him one day—streaked with ash, meeting fellow confused souls on the ghats and telling them about my banking days. That would be a sad end to my odyssey, I thought. But then, maybe not. This dude's eyes shone with obvious pleasure and contentment. He looked… he looked almost happy, although it could well have been the ethereal lights from the remaining diyas.

Still, I was intrigued. He obviously knew something I didn't know. I racked my brains wondering how to sustain the conversation. He appeared completely comfortable and calm in the silence.

Finally, for fear of losing him, I asked, 'Pardon me for asking but I thought I saw you come out from behind the funeral pyre. Was I mistaken or were you praying there or something?'

'Or something,' he replied vaguely. I looked at him puzzled. I wasn't expecting him to be evasive. What could you possibly be hiding when you are buck-naked and smeared with ash? 'What were you doing there if I may ask?' I pressed, expecting to hear about some complicated Indian prayer that helps achieve salvation.

He replied nonchalantly, 'I was hunting for flesh. Fingers, to be specific. Those are my weakness, very delicious. I finally found some that were not charred by the fire, and am carrying them with me now. Do you want to see one?' I was stunned, convinced he was either a psychopath or a lunatic or both. I was planning my escape now. He must have sensed my panic because he continued calmly, 'Look, I don't expect you to understand—your sphere of comprehension is very different. I'm a part of the

Aghoree sect, which you probably haven't heard of. Don't worry, we are not going to sacrifice you or kill you or something.'

I was hardly reassured. 'What is the Aghoree sect?' I asked, curious despite myself.

He replied, 'Aghorees wander from place to place looking for human remains because that is all we eat. We believe that everything that comes from God is an expression of his love and beauty. By feasting on the darkest, most repulsive of His creations, charred human remains, we show our devotion to all creation.'

By now, I was shivering with fear, and my terror grew when I saw one more Aghoree baba, his body smeared with ash as well, walking towards us. Maybe he had a toe fetish or a tongue fetish. I didn't care to find out. 'Jai Shambu Baba. I must take your leave now. It is late—you can keep the rest of the cigarettes,' I said. The white baba smiled an eerie smile as I almost ran from there, convinced that I had encountered a crazed cult of lunatics. Serves me right for wandering around stoned so late in the night, I thought to myself as I rode through the empty streets, trying hard to stay calm and not fall off my bike.

Back at home, I shakily downed several pegs of Scotch to calm my nerves. Soon, curiosity got the better of me and I went on the internet, connecting via the excruciatingly slow dial-up that

I had installed in the room. I searched with various combinations of Aghoree and found that the sect was concentrated around Benares because of the easy availability of human remains there. In fact, the white Aghoree baba I had just met had a couple of websites dedicated to him. He was a minor celebrity whose life had been the subject of a grotesquely titled documentary called *An American Cannibal in Benares*. I would have made a particularly good dinner, I thought, since I had become really fat on rich Indian food in the last year. For all my confusions, ending as a value meal (zero procurement cost) for a bunch of ash-smeared yogis was hardly the solution I was seeking. My nocturnal wanderings did slow down significantly after the incident, although it didn't make me stop getting stoned at the ghats. Only now, I did so in broad daylight and full public view, the fear of flesh-eating babas far outweighing that of being sodomized in a prison cell.

Apart from such sudden, freak encounters though, my days were happy for the most part. To my surprise, even my work delighted me. Until then, I had rarely thought of work as an enterprise anyone could be truly passionate about, but somehow I fell in love with the mad, bad world of retail in India.

At first, my team of hardened salesmen was openly sceptical about my presence and had mockingly nicknamed me 'management' (another one to add to my Indian collection— *'firangi'*, 'toilet paper' and the worst of the lot, 'Dallas', from the 1978 porn movie *Debbie Does Dallas*). I was young, with no sales experience at all, and spoke with a funny accent that they had heard only in the porn movies they saw regularly in a ramshackle movie hall that specialized in screening, illegally of course, the latest hard porn from the US. In a fit of sexual frustration, I saw a movie there once with my sales team. It was disguised as a religious film and devotional songs played in the background as they showed a multiracial orgy involving black, white, Hispanic and Asian actors in hapless, frenzied copulation. My fascinated team assailed me with the usual reactions: 'Sir, you from America, you must have done this all. You live really good life', 'Sir, what is the maximum number you have done in one time?'

New management trainees came from the IIM all the time. They organized team meetings, practised the latest jargon on the increasingly cynical team— 'have a big vision', 'deconstruct the problem', 'broaden your perspective'—came up with new, impractical motivational methods like team anthems every morning, and mostly busied themselves e-mailing pictures to the company's headquarters taking all the credit for their team's fledgling successes. They sincerely applied all the fluff they learnt at business school, but rarely hit the dirt and grime of the market, almost never accompanying the sales guys on their daily calls to the retailers. After all, they had gone to India's top B-school to live the high life. Wasn't it enough of a sacrifice already to be in the dilapidated two-room sales office on a street where you invariably ended up stepping on piles of dog, pig and cow shit, which immediately took the shine away from your newly acquired Gucci shoes (and from life overall, if you came to think of it)?

My team's experiences with B-school trainees made me a persona non grata from the moment I arrived. I overheard many snide comments about myself, comments I was meant to overhear, such as, 'Looks like they have run out of Indians to send. Let's see how quickly we break this bastard.'

Uncharacteristically, this rejection didn't faze me. I knew I would be different from my predecessors, not because of any great desire to excel, but because perversely, the dirt and the grime of the market was what attracted me the most.

Soon, I would go on to enjoy the trip of riding my bike stoned in the crowded lanes, spending hours meeting wholesalers and retailers and diligently observing the well-oiled, complex machinery of retail in India. I would watch fascinated as my sales team negotiated with retailers trying desperately to meet their month-end targets. '*Seth*, I'm finding it difficult to meet this month's number. Can you take an extra case of Kalyan Sanitary Napkins please?' Wholesaler replies: 'Motherfucker, last time's extra cases are still around. You had given the same spiel then. First get those out.' Salesman: 'Just take some extra for this month please. I will give you extra cash the moment I get next month's display budget. You can send Bittoo to Thailand.'

Hmm… so this is where the company's carefully allocated money for 'in-store displays' went— funding a Benares wholesaler's delinquent son's sexual romp in Bangkok. I felt sorry for the suits, who spent hours agonizing and intellectualizing and creating presentations over display-budget allocations in the corporate headquarters. I would see small-town retailers queue up to buy our stuff from the wholesalers, negotiating for every paisa in the vilest language possible: 'Sir, isn't there any scheme or discount for us? I buy so much from you, and you never give me anything special.' Wholesaler turns his back and shows his ass. 'Why don't you take my ass? That will be the only special thing which can satisfy you now. I have gone bankrupt giving you schemes, and yet you keep asking me every time for more and more offers. I can't give a paisa more. I have squeezed everything I can from my own margin.'

Small retailer knows how to play this big game. He says quietly, 'Sahib, Taureef wholesaler is giving a new 12+1 scheme (one pack free with 12 packs). I might have to go there now.' Wholesaler: '*Abey*, that Taureef is a *behenchod*. How many years have you been doing business with me? He is an upstart who won't be around tomorrow. What will you do then? I will fuck you then, and won't even let you buy from me, leave alone give you a scheme.'

The bargaining would go on through the day, each and every rupee being bitterly fought for. Observing these negotiations, one would have thought that a typical wholesaler in India is a cash-strapped destitute. In reality though, being a big wholesaler is an extremely lucrative proposition, and many of the wholesalers I dealt with in Benares were actually closet millionaires. Driving a hard bargain and saving every cent they could was in their blood. Not unlike the investment bankers I worked with on Wall Street, money was the wholesaler's life and getting a good deal their only real dharma.

Ironically, the one exception I knew to this pattern was the king of all Benares wholesalers, the biggest and richest of them all, Raja Bhaiya. He had diversified early in his career after striking it rich as a wholesaler and now ran several other businesses, mostly illegal. On hearing that a new team leader for Shivam Chemicals had come from the US, Raja Bhaiya invited me to meet him for a drink. Much was said about his colourful personal life. A man who lived by his own rules, Raja Bhaiya had a pet white tiger in his backyard, kept several wives and mistresses who lived with him in his vast, sprawling haveli in Old Benares, and had an eye for the arts—every artist who came to Benares had a private showing for Raja Bhaiya before any public performance.

His reason for courting me was simple. Like a modern-day Gatsby, Raja Bhaiya prided himself on his diverse social gatherings, and a US-born B-school graduate working for a big multinational was an interesting specimen to add to his collection. He was always at his most polite with me, and constantly probed me for information about the US.

'What to do, Samrat sir? I had a lot of desire to go to the US, but my visa got rejected. *Kaafi jack lagaya*, but these things are not in the hands of Indian officials. Maybe you can help me?' Raja Bhaiya also turned out to be my informal mentor in the Indian sales world, imparting valuable, unsolicited lessons. 'Samrat sir, the problem with your company is that they have no consistent standards. In sales, if you bend once we will make you bend again. If you are flexible once, we will break your back for even more flexibility. So your salespeople made an exception once by routing display money to us—we now push them to do so every time. Look at P&G. They stick to the principles. We may bitch all the time because they don't give as much money, but we know what we see is what we get. Fair and square. Over the long term that wins, you know. *Chalo* sir, enough of this. Let's see Tony the tiger.'

He was very proud of his white tiger, a rare, majestic animal whose roars could be heard through the house. 'It's a fine animal, Samrat sir. The only white tiger owned privately in India. Me and the tiger, we are like one another. We both rule the jungle—we have everybody under our power yet we roam alone.' Loneliness and death were his greatest fears and he kept bringing these up in our time together. Several times, he made an overt offer to procure drugs or women for me. 'Samrat sir, why do you live alone? I run other businesses besides soaps and shampoos. You give me a chance—I deal in high-quality stuff only.' But I kept our relationship purely professional.

Thanks to Raja Bhaiya's able mentorship though, I was able to make an immediate impact in Shivam's business as I created several sales-driving incentive schemes which changed the dynamics of the stagnant market. This led to more consumers trying our shampoo—many of them for the first time—since surveys showed that almost 50 per cent of women in India had never used a shampoo. I found it gave me a bizarre sense of satisfaction that a woman somewhere in rural India, who defined her life only by her husband and children, had an intimate personal experience when she used the fragrant, international-quality shampoo our company made. It wasn't like Edison inventing the light bulb, but it was infinitely more satisfying than my banking job where all I did was acquire money for rich people, whose troubled lives were made even more troubled by the money I made them. Combined with the incredible experience of getting stoned every day at work, it made me enjoy my job so much that there was never a dull moment in those two months.

Soon enough, my sales team started grudgingly respecting my business ideas though my personal life remained a puzzle for them. They had heard unconfirmed rumours of my running in the streets like a madman every night, of smoking up at the ghats and of alliances with Raja Bhaiya, but I never responded to their inquisitiveness, keeping details of my personal life very much to myself.

Finally, one evening it dawned on me that there was only a week left for the summer internships to end. I felt a pang of despair. I had created the illusion of a life here and I felt miserable at it being snatched away from me. I didn't want money, fame, power or any other transient glory. I just wanted a simple, trivial life like the one I was leading right now, enjoying the little pleasures that life sent my way, drifting on rudderless without ambition and staking my own small claim to happiness. I was happy now, and I could hardly say that so absolutely for any other time in my life. Desperately, I tried to hang on to the sense of perfect, complete solitude in my last week there. I planned for solitary jogs in the mornings, elaborate lonely meals, stoned aartis on the ghats and midnight jaunts on my bike.

It wasn't meant to be. Shine Sarkar decided to grace me with an unannounced trip to Benares before we headed back to Bangalore. 'How could I not come, man? Your letters made me want to drop my internship and come here immediately. And then, the way we parted at the IIM. I wanted to clarify things.' He had completed his internship with Deutsche Bank in London a week earlier than scheduled. Even the workaholic, ball-busting investment bankers had run out of excuses to keep him any longer as he consistently exceeded expectations on everything they threw at him. So he had decided to drop in on me and, with the uniquely Indian sense of entitlement, had given me no notice whatsoever.

As expected, his presence caused a whirlwind of activity, and my last few days in Benares passed in a haze. On my last evening there, I found myself enjoying my last aarti on the banks of the Ganga with Sarkar. Earlier in the day I had been given a satisfyingly tearful farewell by my sales team—'Sir, you were the best. Please stay here with us, we will fuck everybody and always be the top territory in the country.'

I was trying to explain to Sarkar how much the internship had meant to me: 'Somehow my experiences here moved me. You know, last week I even managed to convince the company to increase the salaries of my sales team by a few thousand rupees. Paltry I know, but it means the world to them. These folks sweat all day running from shop to shop, going well beyond their call of duty despite earning less than what I make as a lowly summer intern. Each of them has their own unique version of the great Indian story—old parents toiling away in drought-stricken villages, sisters to marry, big aspirations for their children with no means to achieve them—you know all that better than I do. Don't get me wrong, they aren't saints, they squander away their meagre earnings on porn, gambling and alcohol, but still we live such a privileged life compared to them. It made me feel genuinely good to make some difference to their lives. Plus the work. I never knew selling shampoo sachets could be meaningful.' I paused. I sounded like a pot-smoking Mother Teresa, which I knew I wasn't. I was a heartless bastard. Despite the squalor and abject poverty I had seen in India over the last year, my concerns had hardly risen above my crippling obsession with myself.

'You do seem different,' he said. 'More settled, perhaps. I think I need to start peddling shampoo too.'

'I'm just stoned right now,' I said. 'How was London?'

Sarkar seemed tormented by his usual demons. 'Brain dead just like everywhere else. Crappy work, pubs, theatre, tea and scones. Felt thoroughly fucked like a… like a cucumber in a woman's prison, as your rednecks say.'

I burst out laughing despite the apparent seriousness of his troubles.

'But I did manage to do some thinking of my own,' said Sarkar shyly.

'Go on,' I said interested.

'Vinod will crow like a rooster in labour when I tell him this, but I think he was right. I'm planning to join my Dad after graduation.'

'Really?'

He nodded. 'The more I think about it, I didn't really want to get into the IIT or the IIM. It was just to prove a point to I don't know who. I don't even hate India that much; I just wanted to run away from here. But I am interested in his business, I think I can expand it, take it places. Anyway, it's better than being fucked everyday in the head in a bank.'

'Plus you'll get to know him,' I said. 'He may not be the ogre you think he is. He seems quite nice from the photographs I have seen in magazines.'

Sarkar shrugged as if to say 'I don't care about him, it's just the business I'm interested in'.

Balls, I thought, like hell you care about growing any business.

'Will he lend us some of his arm candy?' I said.

'Hey, look!' Sarkar exclaimed suddenly. At three corners of the banks of the Ganga, three activities were occurring simultaneously, each oblivious of the other. A small child's hair was being shaved for the first time in a *mundan*, signifying his liberation from the burden of his past lives; a young couple was getting married around a holy fire, sacred vows celebrating their entry into a new life; and last rites were being performed on a corpse, its cremation signifying escape from the current life. Birth, marriage, death. It was as if an unknown, powerful force was playing out the whole cycle of life in front of us. 'Look,' the force seemed to be mocking us, 'this is all there is to it.' The scene lodged itself in my mind and as I replayed it in my head, I realized the futility of striving for any more. Everything will be just fine, I think, I had lived a life in that moment.

11

Everything Will Be Just Fine

My fall began with the 'Reorientation' session held immediately after we came back from our summer internships. The human resources faculty at the IIM conducted the programme to force students to reflect on their personal, non-academic learning in the first year at the institute and focus on what they could do differently in the second year to get the most out of their time there. Like most people, I thought it would be fluff.

'Motivational talks and mass reflections won't change anything. The system is too far gone for that. Plus, no one will be honest. Who wants to openly admit how fucked they really are? It's gonna be another "Don't worry, you are all special" sob fest. I don't know about you, but I don't want IIM's help to untap my spiritual potential,' said Sarkar at the beginning of the session, and proceeded to spend the rest of the week catching up on sleep after our Benares escapades. Vinod had gone a step further and decided to give the session a complete miss, spending his time at home instead. 'I'm exhausted, need to think things through after my two-month Singapore jaunt,' he said. I had to confess that I had an inordinate interest in such soul-baring exercises, and I decided to bare it to anyone who cared to listen for the week. Turned out I wasn't alone.

In the very first programme, they called alumni to reflect on their time at school. While we had our share of hackneyed yawn-inducing speakers giving us the 'Make the best of your time at IIM—these are the best days of your life, learn and grow' routine, there were some who were surprisingly insightful. Like the aggressive young investment banker from Mumbai. 'How many other investment bankers have come to give this talk today?' he asked. 'None, right? I will tell you why—they are all busy making money as I should be. Do I love my life? No. I lead a dog's life, but you know what, every January when I get my bonus, it is all justified. Every time I fly to a session like this in the corporate jet, life seems all right, and I'm motivated to work like a dog once again. I have learnt that it is fine to love these gross, material things if that is what you care about. If I have any advice for you, it's this: don't spend your precious time here studying finance or marketing or human resources, none of that will come in use when you start working. Spend your time trying to figure who you are instead—what makes you tick, what you want from life, what makes you happy. The worst off in business school are those who don't spend enough time reflecting on these things here. Every year a few of these losers are seduced by the glamour of banking. What happens then? They come, they see and they leave with their tails between their legs. They don't survive because they haven't figured out that money doesn't do squat for them. They want to live a balanced life, pursue their hobbies, spend time with their families and other such vague niceties which bankers shouldn't be wasting their time on. Of course, they are fired. Corporate life is not the place to find yourself, no one cares there. Now is the time to do that, and so many of you are wasting time studying instead.'

He was crude and arrogant but refreshingly straightforward. Quite his opposite was the soft-spoken, bearded advertising agency owner from Bangalore. 'I wasn't ever the aggressive sort, and frankly, I didn't have a good time at the IIM. It was too intense for me, but I guess something worked out right after all. Way back in 1986, there were two girls in our batch. I married one of them and we set up an advertising agency in Bangalore. It's been fifteen years now. We are not the best or the biggest in the country, but we get by. I'm happy, and really have no advice for you because I guess I define happiness differently from what business school would teach you. If you were really to force me to say something I would just say this—accept who you are and don't try to be like your next-door neighbour. The only judgement that matters is yours; the only one who needs to respect you is you.'

All of them had some version of the same advice that I intuitively believed in, but was glad to hear it from folks who had lived it. Ten years from now, none of my present concerns would matter. Would I care whether I learnt finance, operations or marketing at the IIM? No. Would I care if I was in the top five per cent or the bottom five per cent of the class? No. The only thing I would care about after graduating from here would be whether I had been happy at school or not. Did I have experiences I would remember? Did I have relationships that would stand the test of time? Did I figure out what I really wanted to do? These would be the only things I would look back at and judge my level of satisfaction or dissatisfaction during my time here.

In the next few days, I received several such insights into myself. I learnt, for example, that I didn't have a single entrepreneurial bone in my body as my entrepreneurship scores hovered at rock-bottom in the series of career inventories that we were asked to fill. All my fantasies—opening a restaurant, starting my own film production company—were just that, happy mirages to chase while trying to escape the reality of being a daily wage-earning corporate drone. When the rubber hit the road, I would do no such thing. I wasn't enough of a risk-taker or, for that matter, engaged enough in life to be bothered about leaving a legacy. I was content to muddle along, dream of glory but not act on it, read books of greatness but never be inspired enough to be the subject of one. But this was me and, as the advertising agency owner from Bangalore had said, the more I learnt to live with myself, the happier I would be.

In all, it had been a good week, I thought as I walked back alone from the common hall to the hostel on the last day of the session. A good *year* in fact, I thought. Rough, maybe, confusing, definitely, but overall, I was actually quite happy in a general sense. Nothing specific, like happy at buying a new car or getting a salary hike, but broader in a vague though more permanent sense. Every day, I was gradually accepting my station in life and learning to be happy with it. I had never been materially ambitious, and the year-end banking bonuses or the fast-track CEO path had never interested me much. I always had to muster up enthusiasm and put on a show of ambition in order to fit in. I had left all of that to come here for undefined, confused reasons. But over the past year in India, I had sensed the existence of a broader world around me. A world in which Rajasthani *banjaaras*, who didn't know where they would be tomorrow, could confidently predict your future, where a businessman spent sixty years in a small ashram in the Himalayas devoted to an important but ultimately elusive quest, where an ash-covered investment banker ate charred toes and fingers for salvation, where the owner of a white tiger, a sprawling haveli and several wives complained of loneliness. In the face of these, my confusion about my identity and about not knowing my calling seemed inconsequential and clichéd, little more than obsessive musings of a self-centred mind. Different strokes for different folks; make mistakes, muddle around, stumble, pick up the pieces, rise again, and ultimately, chart your own course.

It was inevitable, therefore, that I spent most of the second year concentrating on more productive activities than academics and lectures. Activities like playing soccer at midnight under the dim lights of the low-wattage bulbs in the IIM courtyard, drunk and stoned out of my mind, for instance. It was Sarkar's idea as usual.

'It's fun—try it, man. Marijuana makes you reflective, alcohol makes you restless, and soccer will force you to concentrate. It won't be a game any more, it will be a spiritual awakening.' There would be days when I would haphazardly try to make sense of the academic curriculum again, but Vinod would convince me otherwise.

'Just let go this year,' he would say. 'Don't succumb to the Superman Syndrome. Have you ever seen Superman stop to think? No, he is always compelled to *act*. Running, flying all the time; he spends as much energy saving the world as capturing a newspaper thief. You don't want to be like that. Don't study just because you *ought* to be studying, it isn't necessary if it isn't necessary.'

Armed with these words of wisdom, I officially 'gave up' in the second year of business school.

Days slipped into months, and the entire second year at the IIM threatened to pass in a haze of marijuana and soccer. Until one day, an encounter in the Reaching Creative Boundaries course set an unexpected chain of events in motion. I had selected the course for much the same reason I had taken all the other electives that year—to expend as little effort as possible and determinedly sleepwalk through classes stoned. As a result, while most of my classmates were studying International Finance and Advanced Corporate Strategy, my course list read like a page from a Kerala meditation spa catalogue, with courses like Discovering Your Inner Leader and Philosophy in Management. On that particular day, the Reaching Creative Boundaries professor had invited a local Kannada author to class for a guest lecture. As with most of his classes, his intent was to push left-brained B-school spreadsheet wizards beyond their comfort zone by exposing them to creativity in flesh and blood.

The author turned out to be a surprisingly sexy, spirited young lady who had quit an indifferent career in advertising to pursue her passion for writing. I was too blown to pay close attention to her lecture, but I liked the slow, measured movement of her lips, the lilting, silken notes in her voice and the animated movement of her hands as she stressed a point. From the few words I heard, she seemed to be encouraging us to have the courage to follow our dreams.

Sure, I thought lazily, but what if I never had a dream? What if I never find anything I can be passionate about? Would I continue to be like this—jaded, cynical and immune to ecstasy? You don't realize how lucky you are to have a dream and a target to chase, however elusive, I thought, as I stared at the inexplicably captivating sight of her pretty lips forming words I couldn't hear.

A sudden buzz of noise in the classroom distracted me. A question had been posed to the author and her soft, melodious voice had turned noticeably harsh as she answered it. I strained to listen.

'It isn't about talent any more,' she said. Apparently, someone had touched a raw nerve by asking her why she wasn't published yet. 'Authors today have to peddle their work as if they are selling aphrodisiacs, underwear and cell phones. Publishers don't want literature any more, they want soft porn, vampire capers and chick flicks disguised as literature.'

B-school had forced capitalism down everyone's throats, so the predictable responses followed.

'What's wrong with that?' someone countered. 'If that's what the market wants, that's what publishers should sell. Let the audience judge what is literature and what isn't.'

'Maybe,' she replied. 'But writing a book isn't like creating a new flavour of toothpaste. At least I like to believe that writing has a higher purpose.'

I paused to consider her point. Her lips quivered with agitation, making her look even sexier. I reflected on the higher calling of writing for a while before I realized, ashamed, that I didn't even care a bit. Who gives a flying fuck, I thought, to each his own. Don't be anyone's moral compass or let anyone be yours. Write porn, write literature or don't write anything at all. Make your choices, stick by them or don't. We are all insignificant drops in the vast ocean of humanity deluding ourselves that our choices made an impact. To live your inconsequential life the best way you know is your only duty, your highest calling.

Chetan raised his hand. 'The highest purpose for a publishing house is to make profits,' he said smugly.

In another life, I would have called him an asshole. Now, he seemed just another guy staking his claim to happiness in the best way he knew. His doggedness was beautiful in its simplicity. Different strokes for different people, I thought.

'Different strokes,' said the author, startling me a little. 'One man's Shakespeare is another man's MC Hammer.'

I think I was a little in love with her by the time the class ended.

I dropped in at Sarkar's room after class that day. He had stopped attending classes altogether, and was lying shamelessly in his now familiar position— sprawled on the bed with a joint in one hand, an obscure philosophy book in the other, psychedelic music playing in the background. I positioned myself on the comfortable mat on the floor. Vinod entered the room just then and I related the events of class that morning. I told them I had fallen in love.

'She is right,' Vinod said unexpectedly. He seemed more interested in the author's view on writing than my views on love. 'Writing should serve a higher purpose. I used to read a lot in the bunkers at Kashmir, mostly fiction, to take my mind off things. Gives you a funny kind of solace, that you are not alone, and someone somewhere thinks exactly like you—and articulates it better.'

I was surprised. I wouldn't have pegged Vinod as a reader; I had barely seen him read his textbooks here.

'I haven't read in a while,' he said reading my thoughts as usual. 'Somehow after the war, fiction began to seem almost frivolous. You must try reading some Indian authors, though, I think you'll like it.' He looked at Sarkar. 'Even though this bastard will tell you that they are trying to be American by writing in English.'

The Indian authors I had read so far had been puzzling in their remoteness. They didn't seem to write about the India I had heard of from Mom and Dad, or the India I had seen in the two years I had spent here. Slow, painful, ten-page reflections on a leaf's colour changing from green to yellow-brown in an Indian fall (I hadn't even noticed fall in Bangalore!), an incestuous Calcutta family in which everybody is fucking everybody, pretentious magic-realism storylines with a river being used as a metaphor for life and assorted clichés—none of it seemed real, interesting or remotely useful (except perhaps to impress a date). Most of it seemed to be written to titillate a fat American wearing cargo shorts, camera hanging down his front, sunning himself belly-up on a beach in Hawaii, reading a book and pontificating on the plight of humanity in developing countries. However, Vinod had recommended them with such genuine emotion that I decided to give it another shot. Plus, I desperately needed help with my love life. If reading poetic descriptions about poverty-stricken Indian youth (as exemplified by Sarkar, no doubt) helped score a date in India, I vowed to become an expert on the subject.

Under Vinod's guidance, I started reading Indian authors I hadn't heard of in the US—to unexpected, startling results. The vague restlessness of Agastya Sen, Upamanyu Chatterjee's slacker, cynical protagonist of *English, August* or the growing pangs of Rusty, Ruskin Bond's delightful underdog from *Delhi is Not Far* were uncannily similar to mine. In them, I found kindred, lost souls who touched me in much the same way that the original misfit of English literature, Holden Caulfield, had. Perhaps I was even more Indian than I thought I was. Or maybe genuine, heartfelt words had a magical, soothing effect no matter where they came from. That twenty years ago an Indian bureaucrat jerking off in a government guest house in rural India was feeling the same sense of dislocation that I was eating sushi in a swanky Manhattan restaurant made me realize that I needn't have come this far to escape my dislocation (although I was glad I did, even if just to realize that I needn't have come).

The Kannada author was right—writing indeed had a higher purpose.

❃

My newfound love for Indian writing did precious little to help my academic pursuits, and fittingly, Vinod, Sarkar and I were smoking up in Sarkar's room when the final grades were released. We were debating whether to make the five-minute journey to the institute building to check on our grades.

Chetan relieved us of our indecision. He came rushing breathlessly to the room and informed us that Sarkar had set a record of sorts for the most dramatic fall in rankings as he slipped from a gold-medal hopeful to well below 100th in the class of 200. This was somewhat expected as the subjects we had selected in the second year weren't math, science or logic-based, and he had no God-given advantage in them. Coupled with my ranking of 160th out of a batch of 180 and Vinod's hovering around the same, our trio cut a very sorry picture indeed.

'What about you?' I asked Chetan.

'Second. Missed it by a whisker,' Chetan said mournfully, referring to the gold medal.

We stared at each other for a few moments after Chetan had gone out of the room, wondering what to think of our shabby performance. Then Sarkar and I looked at each other and burst into sudden laughter. The same thought had crossed our minds.

'Really,' Sarkar said, 'is there any difference between being second in the batch or 160th? Neither of us gets the gold medal. Bastard just wasted his two years.'

'Unlike us, who spent it so productively,' quipped Vinod with a luxurious wave of his hand around Sarkar's room where an unfinished joint rested in an ashtray, empty bottles of rum, vodka and whiskey stood against the walls and unopened textbooks lined the shelves.

We collapsed into more laughter. One thing led to another and Vinod, the devoted Bollywood addict, coerced us into celebrating our magnificent academic performance by going for a movie that night. ('They are playing an Amitabh Bachchan classic,' he said. 'Have you ever seen one? It's a life-changing experience.') I agreed to change my life on the condition that we smoke all our remaining joints to prepare for the three hours of mindlessness.

The joints had their desired effect. Soon, the mad cacophony of sights and sounds in the movie theatre became pleasantly tolerable. Flashes of colour lit up the screen. The comfortable boom of the onscreen dialogue resounded in my ears. I could feel the uneven contours of the torn seat below me and became acutely aware of my arm resting on the warm armrest. The Pepsi tasted sticky and sweet. From the corner of my eye, I saw Vinod staring at the screen with a look of absolute contentment on his face. I turned to look at Sarkar, who was carefully examining every kernel of popcorn he picked up from his bag. I felt a sudden rush of warmth towards them. My two-year Indian odyssey is over, I thought in a vague, distracted way. I would graduate in a week. Could I really go back to my old life?

I spaced out trying to focus on the problem when suddenly an onscreen dialogue from Amitabh Bachchan, the legendary superstar, caught my attention.

'*Hum jahan pe khade ho jaate hein, line wahin se shuru hoti hai,*' said Amitabh dramatically as he cut the queue of washed-up goons waiting for food in a prison cell. He stood tall at the head of the line. 'The queue begins where I stand.'

When all else fails, trust in Amitabh Bachchan.

12

The Queue Begins
Where I Stand

I made my weekly call to my parents after returning to the hostel that night.

'Have you decided what you are doing next?' my father asked immediately, though his tone was less reproachful than usual—or perhaps I was not listening for disapproval this time.

'I just called up Goldman before I called you,' I said.

He heaved an audible sigh of relief. 'So you are coming back then?'

'Yes,' I said. 'But not to their investment banking division. They have a newly created philanthropic arm that leads microfinance solutions for developing countries. No one wants to go there, as you can imagine, so there are a ton of leadership positions open. It pays much less, but I think I will be happier there.'

I waited for the protests—but there was none.

'Are you sure you want to do this?' he said evenly.

'You know my views about charity. First help yourself, then help others, get something before you give it away.'

'I know *your* views, Dad,' I smiled. 'But *mine* have evolved a bit in India.'

Earlier, I would have shut off assuming he would never understand, but today I felt compelled to explain—maybe because I didn't feel as if I was justifying or rationalizing.

'I'm kind of tired of living this self-obsessed, Johnny-stuck-in-a-bubble life, you know; all I have thought about thus far has been *my* needs, *my* desires, *my* pleasure, *my* sorrow, *my* wins, *my* losses. I kind of liked it in Benares where I felt I was doing something for someone for a change, however insignificant. I just don't want to keep trying to win a race that I don't even want to run in the first place,' I said.

'There will be enough time for self-actualization later,' he said. 'Don't make choices in your youth that you'll regret your whole life.'

'I don't think I will regret it,' I said. 'And honestly, in the broad world order, it's less important a move than Britney Spears shaving off her hair or Lindsay Lohan checking into rehab.'

'Who?' he said.

'Never mind. My point is I am still working finance in Wall Street, just using my skills in a different—and I think better—way. The division is new and I could give it a lot of direction from the little bit I have seen of India as a developing country,' I said. 'I don't know, Dad, it just feels right this time.'

'Well, your life,' he said. 'We are just glad you are coming back.'

'Don't worry too much, Dad,' I said. 'As they say here: *Zindagi apne raaste khud hi dhoondh leti hai.* Life has a way of finding its own way.'

'When in doubt, use flexible Indian philosophy,' he said. He paused. 'You do sound different, though.

'Different how? Is the Indian accent more pronounced?' I said.

He laughed. 'No, I mean, more silent, more grown-up, perhaps,' he said. 'I feel slightly more confident of your decisions.'

'I don't know about that,' I said as I saw Sarkar with a brown paper bag in his hand gesturing for me to hurry up so we could kick-start the night.

'You sounded happier in India, so much so that we were worried you wouldn't want to come back,' he said.

'I'd be happy anywhere now that I am done running from myself for a while,' I said.

Sarkar looked as if he was about to break into the booth. 'Ironically, I have to rush now, though,' I said.

I came out of the booth feeling an irrepressible, irrational joy. I could be whoever I wanted to be, I thought, doing whatever I chose to do. Like

Amitabh Bachchan, I was right at the head of this race—of one.

'Now that the good doctor is taken care of, let's get started, shall we?'

I wanted to accompany him, but I also wanted to be completely alone. In India, everything is true and its opposite is true as well.

'Sure,' I said. 'But I'm gonna go slow on the funk.'

'Hell, no!' he said. 'Not another of your turns coming on.'

But I felt giddy enough anyway. Tonight, I would just keep off the grass.

Acknowledgements

My special thanks to some awesome folks who changed the trajectory of my life, a little bit at a time, and made it pretty rocking fun:

Rupa Sharma, for believing when necessary and doubting when absolutely required; I owe the book's completion to you.

Mom and Dad—for your unconditional support always.

Sonali and Avneesh Arya for being more friends than family—and for providing absolutely terrific inputs to the first novel you read in your lives!

Hinoti Joshi; once a colleague, now a dear friend. Thanks for all your help and generosity. I think you rock.

My editors at HarperCollins—Karthika V.K., Shantanu Ray Chaudhuri, Neelini Sarkar. Thanks for turning this into a novel I can be (mostly) proud of.

Renuka Chatterjee and Kavita Bhanot from Osian's Literary Agency; for caring as if it were your own creation.

Bhaskar, Werner from Pink&White Consulting, Lipika, Dev, Debargha Basu; for going way beyond what was necessary.

The Indian Army, BIT Mesra, IIM Bangalore, P&G—awesome institutions—and some of my terrific mentors there: Shailesh Jejurikar, J.P. Kuehlwein, Maile Carnegie, to name just a few.

My friends from various phases of my life. I know I am judgmental sometimes, opinionated most of the time, and cynical almost always. So I feel lucky to be blessed with such unconditionally caring friends. My special thanks to Saurabh 'Tiger' Nanda, first reader, friend, philosopher, critic, believer; Vinod Raghuwanshi, Somak Dhar and Jason Chrenka—all of you will unwittingly find yourselves thrust in the middle of these pages (go sue me!). Dushyant, Tarun, Shaira, Ajay-gand, Naidu, Hapur, Sid J-Chipps and Koyal, Palthi, Rohan, Madhur, Trupti, Alex and many others—for reading, providing inputs and believing. But mostly, thanks for years and years of rocking, life-changing friendships. Friendship is often an under-appreciated bond, and I want to use this space to say that you mean the world to me.

Finally, my thanks as a fan to Upamanyu Chatterjee and Ruskin Bond who unknowingly taught me the power of writing. If my book can touch even one person the way *English*, *August* or *Delhi is Not Far* touched me, the number of trees felled to print this would be justified somehow!